Sons of the 43rd:

The Story of Delmar Dotson, Gray Allison, and the Men of the 43rd Bombardment Group in the Southwest Pacific

Michael R. Spradlin, PhD

Published by
Innovo Publishing, LLC
www.innovopublishing.com
1-888-546-2111

Providing Full-Service Publishing Services for
Christian Authors, Artists & Organizations: Hardbacks, Paperbacks,
eBooks, Audiobooks, Music & Film

SONS OF THE 43RD:
THE STORY OF DELMAR DOTSON, GRAY ALLISON,
AND THE MEN OF THE 43RD BOMBARDMENT GROUP IN THE SOUTHWEST PACIFIC

Library of Congress Control Number: 2016954455
ISBN: 978-1-61314-351-3

Cover Design & Interior Layout: Innovo Publishing, LLC
Printed in the United States of America
U.S. Printing History

First Edition: November, 2016

Dedication

To Carrie Lee Nelson, Brenda Dotson Salyers, and Lynda Hubbard.
The ones who kept the family flame alive.

Endorsements

"This book is story telling and military history at its best. Mike Spradlin has professionally researched and superbly written this smooth flowing home front/aerial combat narrative. He writes with incredible insight bringing life to these brave airmen of the Greatest Generation and their loved ones back home, who can no longer speak for themselves. *Sons of the 43rd* is an outstanding military historical book. A great read and a real page turner to the end."

Henry B. "Sonny" Tucker, LTC USA (ret.), Cdr., Hill 65, 8 November 1965, RVN…Silver Star.

A book that illuminates and excites, then reminds us there is still much to learn about WWII in the Pacific. Mike Spradlin tells the story of our greatest generation with warmth and feeling, where we see that these young men were asked to do things on a daily basis that no airman or soldier would tolerate in today's military. A must read for anyone interested in WWII, the Pacific Arena or the personal sacrifices of war. Excellent on many levels.

Susan Clark Lanson, President 43rd Bomb Group Association

"They have been called the greatest generation—that hardy, self-reliant group that came to their nation's aid in its time of greatest need. This is their story and how they were challenged and honed for the fight ahead and ultimately prevailed. Seen through the eyes of TSgt Delmar Dotson, a B-17 flight engineer and top turret gunner, and Lt. Gray Allison, a B-24 pilot, this is the personal story of the airmen who were the 43rd Bomb Group, that hardy group who General Kenny threw into the breech to staunch the threatened invasion of Papua New Guinea and Australia in the desperate summer of 1942. It is a very personal story that suitably honors all members of the 43rd Bomb Group who answered their nation's call."

Lt Gen Walter E. Buchanan III, USAF (ret) whose father lived this story as a 43BG B-17 bombardier, '42-'43.

"Every American family was touched by the Second World War in some way. Many had sons, brothers, sisters, daughters—even fathers or mothers—serving in uniform. Others demonstrated their commitment to the war effort on the home front by other means, such as organizing scrap metal and paper drives, planting Victory gardens and donating blood. Many of those who actually fought in combat lived to tell about it and often did so. Yet countless numbers of these veterans never spoke of their wartime ordeals to anyone. Regrettably, almost 300,000 American men and women who fought in World War II never survived to tell their stories. For them, that was left up to curious individuals or family friends and relatives—Michael Spradlin, as in Delmar Dotson's case—to do it for them.

"'War is hell.' So said General William T. Sherman nearly 100 years before the men and crews of the 43rd found themselves in a far flung corner of the South Pacific battling against a fierce and determined Japanese military machine. The various accounts of what these airmen and their support personnel endured—poisonous snakes, biting and stinging insects, sweltering heat, unbearable humidity, malaria and other tropical diseases—give much credence to General Sherman's observation about war. Yet, through it all, the men of the 43rd persevered. Despite doubt and disappointment, they never wavered. In spite of losses and failures, they never gave in nor gave up. While the world was at its very worst, TSgt Delmar Dotson and the other valiant men of the 43rd epitomized its very best.

"What makes *Sons of the 43rd: The Story of Delmar Dotson, Gray Allison, and the Men of the 43rd Bombardment Group in the Southwest Pacific* such an interesting read is that Michael Spradlin's painstaking and detailed research, which he weaves into a captivating narrative, brings Delmar Dotson and the crew of their ill-fated B-17 *Listen Here, Tojo!* back to life. Far more important than the span of their time in theater, Michael Spradlin gives us behind the scenes glimpses of the men, their backgrounds, their personalities and their character. In doing so, we not only get to know them, but in a sense, become one with them. Now seventy-odd years after WWII ended, thanks to Michael, even though many have forgotten the members of the 43rd Bombardment Group, many shall long remember."

Col. Alan J. Murray (ret.), Meritorious Service Medal, Order of Daedalians, pilot, and currently ACM, FlightSafety, Int'l.

Contents

Preface

One of my earliest family memories is of my grandmother, Laura Dotson Spradlin, reliving when her brothers and sister were given away to an orphanage due to a family tragedy. Other than her pain, the story meant little to me at the time. Later I learned that one of the "orphan children"—Delmar Dotson—died in World War II in the last B-17 lost in the Pacific Theater of war.

When Delmar's plane was discovered in the mountains of New Guinea in the early 1990s it became apparent that many of the events of his life had been lost to the family memory. Delmar never married and had lived away from his family for most of his life. The lack of records made learning anything about his life or military service difficult. Over the years, I began to research and gather data as a matter of personal curiosity at first. As a student of all kinds of history, I've tried to select a few individuals for study and "walk in their shoes" as much as possible. I decided to do this with my great-uncle Delmar Dotson.

Most of my career has been in a church or academic setting, and one of the people I've worked closest with has been Dr. B. Gray Allison. He was the president of my alma mater when I attended graduate school, and then I followed him as the school's second president. I knew he was a veteran of World War II and had flown bombers in the Pacific, and I had collected his war anecdotes through the years on the rare occasions when he felt like talking. It was only after knowing him for thirty years that I picked up the phone and said, "5th Air Force, 43rd Bomb Group, 65th Squadron" to which he replied, "That was my unit." It had been Delmar's unit as well.

In my research, I learned that one of Delmar's crewmates on his silver-star mission had lived in my own city of Memphis, Tennessee. Lt. Col. Max Mayer, US Air Force, ret., alas, died a few years before I learned of his connection to Delmar or of his service to our nation. One is reminded that as the World War II generation passes on, we are losing an irreplaceable resource—the Greatest Generation.

Delmar fought at the beginning of the war in the Pacific, and Gray fought at the end. Their service may not have been pivotal, but it was typical. I hope that their story will remind us of the valiant unnamed heroes of our nation, and I hope that this work will contribute to the anecdotal style of history that I love so much.

Acknowledgments

Many people have assisted in this project, first and foremost, Terrence N. Brown, Director of the Library at Mid-America Baptist Theological Seminary. The great staff at the Air Force Historical Research Agency, especially Miranda Gilmore, provided valuable assistance and documentation. Music historian Harry B. Soria of Hawaii was of assistance for the prewar years when Delmar was in the 27th Infantry Regimental band. Brenda Dotson Salyers, publisher of Heritage Nook Books, and her sister Lynda Hubbard helped me understand the history of southwest Virginia and the Dotson family. Finally, Delmar's little sister, Carrie Lee Nelson, generously gave of her time, letters, and pictures to make the story complete. Numerous websites have been established to document the deeds of the men and women of the Pacific Theater in World War II, and their sites are invaluable starting places for information and anecdotes.

Prologue

The senator's wife had the dream again. Carrie Lee Nelson, wife of Senator Gaylord Nelson of Wisconsin, lost her big brother, Delmar Dotson, over New Guinea in World War II. His plane flew into a cloud and was not heard from for fifty years. Since his mysterious disappearance in 1943, she had often dreamed of him. Delmar had been her protector as they grew up together in the orphanage, and she had taken his disappearance hard. Sometimes at night she would dream of them as youths with their lives ahead of them. The dream was never an omen but seemed more of a question.

The dream was always the same: Carrie Lee is a young nursing student on the sidewalks of Richmond, Virginia, and Delmar walks by in his khaki uniform, strong and tall. He looks ahead unseeing and won't answer her playful calls to him. She wakes up asking, "Where are you, brother?" This book is the answer to your question, Aunt Carrie Lee.

Chapter One:

DELMAR DOTSON'S EARLY LIFE

"We started a good business of good food and clean rooms."
—Lola Dotson, 1920

Delmar Dotson's people had been in the mountains of Southwest Virginia a long time. The area of Pound, Virginia—known as "the Pound" to the locals—had been traversed by Native Americans for centuries before the English settlers started moving in just after the Revolutionary War.[1] Remoteness and hardship were realities as much as the steep mountains around them. The few precious resources were husbanded with great care as was the hope for a better life. The people of the mountains, and the people of the few precious swaths of bottomland, valued hard work and family. Delmar's story begins with them.

DIED IN THE WAR: SEPTEMBER 1863

Tandy Branham was missing a horse, and he knew who had taken it. Alf Killen and the Yankee Home Guards of the 39th Kentucky Mounted Infantry had passed through the Pound, Virginia, area and stolen Tandy's horse from his farm hand, Spence. Killen's "Home Guard" unit was notorious for their thievery and violence. On one occasion, Killen passed by the home of Isom Mullins and tried to buy one of Mullins' horses. When Mullins refused to sell the horse, Killen shot it. On this occasion, Killen and Joel D. "Dusty Pants" Long stole Tandy's horse and then set up in the bushes alongside the road and waited for Branham to come after them.

Tandy, popular with both Union and Confederate sympathizers in the region, set off alone to retrieve his stolen property. The area in which he lived, the Pound, sat near the border of Virginia, Tennessee, and Kentucky, so cross-border raids during the American Civil War were commonplace. He may have ridden alone because so many men were off fighting the war. Tandy mounted his horse on this September 25, 1863 day to follow the marauders, figuring he could track them and take care of his business well enough. Stealing a man's horse was more than a wartime raid; it was a personal matter and horses were more precious than ever in these times. Besides, Tandy could not abide a horse thief.

He knew that the Yankees had traveled near South of the Mountain, since good roads were hard to find in the hills and hollows of Southwest Virginia. What Tandy didn't know was that Killen and his men were waiting for him in ambush. Killen hoped that stealing the horse would flush out Branham, and he and his men waited for their moment. They set up along the road in a place that gave them good cover and a field of fire. These men, probably from Company F or Company K of the 39th Kentucky, were well experienced by this date in the war in the art of bushwhacking.

As Tandy came through the mountains, he rode right into the ambush. Killen's men waited until he came into range and then they shot him down. Even with the primitive guns of the Home Guard units, one man against a crowd never left much room for hope. The Yankees left with Tandy's horse to ride back to Kentucky, and they left the dead body of Tandy Branham along the road in the Virginia-Kentucky pass.[2]

Tandy's five-year-old son, Wilburn, called Wib by his family, never forgot seeing his dead father brought into his house that 1863 day. Some men had found Tandy's body on the road and tied a sheet to some rails and carried the body home in the makeshift stretcher. While the men stood in the house with the bullet-riddled body of the boy's father, Wib remembered watching the blood dripping to the floor. Standing by the pool of her husband's blood, Wib's mother prepared the body for burial. Wib and his older brother, unused to the work of grownups, now dug the grave and, along with their mother, laid Tandy Branham to rest.

James Monroe Roberson of Wise County, Virginia, recalled a boyhood memory of that September day:

> The first thing I call to mind during the Civil War was when I was wearing a red flannel dress at the home of my uncle, Martin Branham, and a turkey gobbler chasing me into the house. I also remember being at the home of Aunt Betty Branham when her husband, Tandy, was brought home a corpse. Some of the Union Home Guard had passed Uncle Tandy's house and had stolen a horse. Uncle Tandy followed them and was killed. They knew Uncle Tandy was a Rebel sympathizer.

In fact, Tandy was more than a Rebel sympathizer, he was the quartermaster for Camp Pound of the Confederate Army. A record of a transaction in the Wise courthouse read:

Camp Pound, Wise County, Va., Feb. 22, 1863
Confederate States of America in account with James M. French, eighty dollars for one sorrel horse.
(Signed) Tandy Branham, A.Q.M. [Adjutant Quartermaster][3]

Rumor had it at the time that Tandy Branham had a large sum of government money in his possession because of his role as an area quartermaster. Perhaps the Yankees wanted more from him than just his horse.

Wilburn "Wib" Branham never forgot the pain of the loss of his father or the lessons of growing up without a dad. Wib knew that the struggle of life must go on. He grew up, married Lou Emma Gilliam, and passed on not only his stories but also his ability to carry on in the midst of tragedy. Soon he and Lou Emma

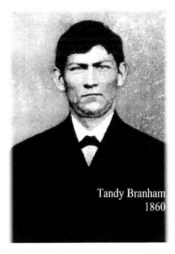

Tandy Branham
1860

Tandy Branham abt. 1860

welcomed their first children into their household, including a beautiful daughter they named Delsie.

Tandy Branham grave 2015

DELMAR'S MOTHER

Delsie Mae Branham was born near Pound, Virginia, at the Whitt Settlement, on October 7, 1885, and was destined to live ninety-seven years, most of them hard ones. In an interview in 1970, when asked how many brothers and sisters were in her family, she quipped, "I'd have to count that" (she had eleven siblings). Delsie's baby brother, Lacy, recalled that they would run around in the summertime without shoes, so Lou Emma would apply cow manure and milkweed as cures for chapped feet. Since Lacy was scared of everything, his sisters, Delsie and Carrie, constantly came to his rescue. Delsie's younger sister Carrie said Lacy and the boys never did any work; the girls even had to chop all the wood. Carrie moaned, "I had to get up early Sunday morning and milk three or four cows and then go to Sunday school at the Pound." They never made the boys do anything.

Wib remained patient with his family, trying to be the father to them that he had not had. The children never remember him saying a cross word to his wife, and he parented them with patience and wisdom. Wib had a reputation for few words, but the same could not be said for his wife, Lou Emma. "Aunt Emma," as many called her, was a shouter. In the church meetings of the day, when the Spirit moved you, you shouted. That was frontier religion, after all. People had hard lives, so when the Lord came down, you gave it all you had with cries of "Hallelujah" and "Glory be." One account said that when Aunt Emma left a particularly good meeting at the Baptist church, she kept up the shouting while Wib walked along, presumably in silence. Wib would walk beside her as she rode their horse to church. He never went inside the church house but waited outside until the meeting was over and then walked Lou Emma home. As Lou Emma kept up the shouting on the ride, Wib may have figured he had enough religion already.

As in every family, sibling rivalries were present as the children grew. Carrie was jealous of sister Delsie because Delsie was the oldest, had her own horse to ride, and could get a boyfriend any time she wanted. Further, Delsie

Young Delsie Branham

Lou Emma Branham,
Old Regular Baptist

Wilburn "Wib" Branham

was allowed to board in the nearby town of Wise and attend the Normal School there. Delsie didn't consider herself so privileged, though. While enrolled at the school, she was under the strict tutelage of the noted (or notorious, depending on your source) school teacher known as Professor Chapman. Delsie thought that Professor Chapman was "the meanest man around," but she stayed through the ninth grade, all that was available at that time.

Now past the ninth grade and preparing for the next phase of her life, Delsie remembered walking to the old Hillman School on Indian Creek where a singing school was being held. A young blue-eyed, brown-haired teenager named Albert Dotson caught her eye. Attending church and church events was more than just encouraged in the Branham household. Lou Emma made sure her children, including Delsie, grew up in the Christian faith, which prompted Delsie to reminisce, "They had religion in those days, young people that is." Albert and Delsie began to see more of each other at church events such as Sunday school. Soon enough, Albert asked Delsie to be his wife.

DELMAR'S FATHER

Delsie sized up Albert Dotson as a man who knew how to take charge of things and wanted to go places in life. He shined his shoes every night to prepare for the next day, even after a long day running the band mill (saw mill). Albert's musical talent included more than singing. He could build anything with his hands, and he made a violin that was played by family members for years. After Albert's proposal, Delsie gleefully told her sister Carrie, "I am going to get married so I don't have to wait on you."

22

Delsie Branham was a June bride in the year of 1905, and soon the sounds of little girls, Lola and Laura, echoed in the home. These girls would grow up with such different personalities that Delsie's friends would later ask her what she had been eating when she was with child with each of them.

In the first years of their marriage, Albert and his brother Jonnie would move to different areas and set up their saw mill for operation. Once the "shanty shacks" were built to house the workers, they started processing the

Albert Dotson

lumber. Albert and Jonnie managed the operation, and Delsie did the cooking for the camp on a wood cook stove. Albert, always looking for new business ventures, moved the family into town and rented a hotel to manage. And the fact that a bear wandered into the Dotson shanty may have further influenced Albert to seek more permanent lodgings.

Daughter Lola recollected that drinking, swearing, or fighting were not allowed in the Dotson household and that Albert always took up for his children. One day Laura crawled under the house chasing the family pig when the pig bit her on the shoulder. Albert was so furious that he shot the pig and "that was the end of that." Oldest daughter Lola also remembered the early days of the family as a time of elegance and clean sheets.

"We moved to Clintwood, Virginia, after a short time. My dad rented the Chase Hotel. We started a good business of good food and clean rooms. Mother was a fantastic cook and manager. We had no plumbing so bowls and pitchers were used in each room along with slop jars (chamber pots), which were hidden under the beds. Each room had wash stands with racks to hold the towel and washcloth. Most of the hotel rooms were beautiful with fancy carpet, nice bedspreads, and fine curtains. Other rooms were plain with just ordinary furnishings. We had a large dining area where food was served. We used white linen table covers and they had to be starched and ironed as slick as a ribbon."[4]

The family grew in addition to Lola and Laura with the first son to come along, Glenn. Then it was Willie (William Albert, Jr.), Virgil, Delmar, Carrie Lee, and Ralph. Delmar Lester Dotson entered the world in June of 1916. Albert, with so many mouths to feed, added the job of Magistrate of Wise, Virginia, to his hotel duties.[5] He also started a shoe shop to even further supplement the family's income.

Wise County and the town of Pound, Virginia, were largely untouched by the Great World War when Delmar Dotson was born. Although his military records would list Delmar as being born in 1918, he was born June 13, 1916, to Albert Dotson and Delsie Branham Dotson, the sixth of eight children. With the introduction of the World War I draft, Albert registered in September of 1918 and listed himself as self-employed and with the occupations of working a hotel and being a merchant in Clintwood, Virginia. His age, thirty-five, kept him from military service. The registration clerk listed Albert as tall and slim with blue eyes and dark hair.

Albert Dotson, Mason, and Shriner

THE MOVE TO KENTUCKY

Soon Albert had his eyes on another opportunity. The proposed town of Jenkins, Kentucky, was planned for just across the Virginia-Kentucky border. This unique place, to be started in 1912 by a combination of lumber, coal, and railroad entrepreneurs, needed business leaders and Albert answered the call. He planned to open a hotel and commissary (store) in Jenkins. Workers began constructing the town as soon as the companies purchased a large-enough area of land. After the property was bought, the combination of coal, lumber, and rail companies announced the construction of the new city, a place of jobs and opportunity, carved out of the wilderness. The rugged conditions and remote location proved a daunting challenge. To build the town of Jenkins, twenty head of oxen pulled locomotive parts over the mountains. A railroad line was carved through the mountains, and buildings were constructed to take care of all of the needs of a community. The nascent town of Jenkins began when its civic leaders officially declared the town open April 20, 1912.[6]

Albert and the family had been doing well in the hotel business. He had purchased one of the first cars in the area, a Ford, and he loved driving the family to different events around town. These automotive adventures lasted until Albert's brother-in-law, who may have had too much to drink to control the new-fangled contraption, wrecked the car. He told his brother he "saw two roads and took the best one." With the risky move to Jenkins to restart their business, the Dotson family, including Delmar, left behind the player piano, the shoe shop and store, and the hotel to move to the new town of Jenkins and set up shop. Presumably the wrecked car stayed behind as well.

Delmar's older sister Laura remembered the days of managing the Jenkins store as good ones. She recalled, "When new dresses would arrive, Father would let me try them on." Delsie bought daughter Laura a fur coat that cost the incredible price of $88.00 to celebrate Laura's new job at one of the shops in town. Laura later loaned the coat to her older sister Lola, who loved looking fashionable. Lola never returned the coat, having told Laura that she lost it. That this was not true was the least of Laura's worries, as bigger troubles lay ahead. The businesses, store and hotel, kept the family busier than ever. Albert had moved on from his saw mill days, but the long hours were grueling. The family frequently had sixty boarders to care for, and as one child remembered, with no plumbing in the building, there were "many buckets to empty every day." Delsie was known for her cooking skills and was fondly remembered for many special dishes, including her special fried squirrel and dumplings.

Laura Dotson

Approaching Storms

When work was done for the day, Albert loved to spend time with Delmar and all of his children. They laughed and carried on until time for bed, and then he would polish his shoes to get ready for another day. But dark clouds were gathering on the horizon for the happy Dotson family. Oldest daughter Lola began seeing a man who was objectionable to her father. Albert, possibly worn down from the years of hard labor, came down with the flu and couldn't seem to get well. Although Lola would always think that she had broken her daddy's heart, the flu would bring on graver consequences. Delsie remembered Albert walking around one night with his shoes untied, and she asked him what was wrong. "Look at my feet and legs." Albert couldn't tie his shoes because of the swelling in his feet. Severe swelling had set in since the flu, and the swelling gradually worked its way up his body.

Albert knew he was in trouble. One night after work, he went straight to bed and was unable to get up. The community nurse, Mrs. Jackson, arrived to examine him, but she left the house with a grim expression on her face. Albert's youngest son, Ralph, was playing in the room beside his dad when Albert called him to the bed and said, "Ten years from now you will never know who your daddy was." Before Albert died, he called his son Willie to his bed and said, "Son, you will have to take care of your mother, brothers, and sisters." Albert's prophecy came true when Willie was forced to go to work in the coal mines at the age of fourteen. To escape the mines, he joined the army at seventeen but left after a year to return and support the family.[7] Why Willie was chosen for this overwhelming task and not older brother Glenn was not remembered in the family stories.

Albert's condition worsened, and no cure seemed able to prevent his oncoming demise. Delsie went up to their bedroom room on a Friday night, and "he was gone." The official cause of death was "heart dropsy." The young boy from Singing School had gone and left her, and now the growing realization of being mother and breadwinner slowly set in on newly widowed Delsie Branham Dotson.

Though Delmar never took the opportunity to write down his memories about the days before his father died, they must have been pleasant if busy. His family was hardworking, churchgoing, and constantly

This hotel was in Gladeville, later renamed Wise (the town). This was also called the Mansion House. This hotel would have been similar to Albert and Delsie's when they lived on Brick Yard Hill in Jenkins, Kentucky.[8]

surrounded with interesting people who stayed in the family hotel. The death of his father would bring more than just sadness to his life; a radically different path would now be set before him. At ten years of age, Delmar was fatherless. Old Wib, Delmar's grandfather, knew well the pain of losing a father. He tried to step in, but there was only so much he could do. Delsie, widowed mother of eight children, was going to have to find a way to feed, clothe, and house this large brood. Years later, Delsie was asked why she never remarried. She gave two reasons. First, "If the Lord took my husband, then I didn't see the need to go get another one." The second reason was because of the never-ending work of single parenting: "I never thought about a man; I was a widow woman with eight children to raise."

As if Albert's death were not enough, daughter Laura said that a fire in the family business further added to the litany of woes for the Dotsons. Though others in the family don't remember the fire, the death of Albert was a financial disaster for the family. Delsie barely kept the boarding house running for the next year and a half, even with every family member doing their part. Daughter Laura recounted, "I had to pack lunches for twenty-two men every day. It was my senior year of high school, and I was paying my own way through school. We had a bakery in Jenkins, and I would stop in after school and get bread and lunch meat and put it in the men's lunches. I would get up early, pack lunches, and then go to school."

At night Laura would study, and little Ralph would look at the pictures in her book while she studied. She would see to Delmar and the others if they needed help. Some of the townsfolk tried to help, like the men of the mining camp, who would come after their shift was over to see if they were all right. Also, the family of Laura's best friend, Victoria Carpenter, would check on them from time to time. Finally giving up the hotel, Delsie moved the family to Mudtown Hill in Jenkins and took in boarders to pay the bills. With the coal mine companies eager for workers, no shortage existed of men needing a place to live.

THE DECISION

What Delsie knew in her heart soon became apparent to others in the community. She wasn't going to make a go of raising a family by herself. As the children came of age, they began to move out on their own, but it wasn't enough. Oldest daughter Lola married the man who broke her daddy's heart and soon realized that Albert had been right all along. The man she married was trouble. The next oldest daughter, Laura, was thinking of marriage to Dewey Spradlin, one of the coal miners in town (who may have been a boarder in their home as well). Dewey's grandfather, recently passed, had fought for the Union in a Kentucky regiment of mounted infantry, though not with the unit that had killed Tandy Branham, their grandfather. Riley Spradlin had worn the blue and fought in these very hills for the Union. Wib apparently never expressed an opinion of this development, one way or the other.

As woe added to woe, son Glenn, always considered the hardest-headed of a stubborn family, was arrested for breaking the Jenkins' town curfew. As soon as he was old enough, he left town to join the army.[9]

That Delmar was hardly mentioned by the family during this time is a testimony to his willingness to work hard and stay out of trouble. He did watch, however, as his idyllic family life continued to unravel.

One Sunday morning, while walking with the children to church and Sunday School at the Pound, Delsie stopped by the old saw mill that Albert used to manage. Albert had had a well dug there, and Delsie went to a nearby house to borrow a dipper to get the children a drink of water from the well of so many pleasant memories. Instead of the dipper, Delsie got a stern lecture from the resident of the house. "What are you going to do with these boys? They'll be hung before they're twenty years old." Continuing on their way, Virgil asked his mother to let them go away from this place. Delmar's thoughts on the confrontation were lost to time.

RESCUE

What the disintegrating Dotson family didn't realize was that help was on the way. The diminished family fortunes were the topic of discussion at one of the area's fraternal organizations, and it was decided that the time for talk was done and immediate intervention was needed. Delsie received a caller who said that some of the men of the community would like to come and visit with her and discuss her current state of family affairs.

In what became the first of a series of conversations, the men of the Masonic Lodge asked Delsie to consider giving up her children. The men told her that a beautiful home and school located in Richmond, Virginia, had been established for orphans and would be perfect for her younger children. "But of course, Mrs. Dotson, you will have to give up your children."

In the good early years, while living in Clintwood, Virginia, Albert Dotson had joined the Masonic Lodge, rising to the rank of a thirty-second degree Mason and then going on to become a Shriner. His Mason's diploma stated that he had been accepted as a "Master of the Royal Secret of the 32nd degree of the ancient accepted Scottish Rite, Clintwood, Virginia, October 9, 1919." After completion of his Masonic degrees, Albert also joined the Ancient Order of the Mystic

Shrine, commonly known as the Shriners. Albert's association with the ancient order of Freemasonry did more than provide fellowship and community involvement; it also made his fatherless children eligible to live in an orphanage known as the Masonic Home of Richmond, Virginia. Children raised at the Masonic Home were clothed, fed, housed, and educated. Perhaps it was time for Delsie to give away her youngest four children so that they could have a better life.

How often the men of the Masonic Lodge came to Delsie is unknown, but she later remembered that someone would mention her need to give up her children when she was at the post office, or anywhere, in town. The men of the lodge met with her on numerous occasions to plead with her to think of her children's best interests and to let the home adopt and raise these poor fatherless waifs. Each time, Delsie answered no, she would raise her children herself, thank you.

The struggles to feed the family continued. Delsie took a job in a sewing factory in Erwin, Tennessee, to earn some more cash, but it wasn't enough. Word came that Delsie's father, Wib Branham, wasn't doing well since his wife Lou Emma's death. It seemed as if the weight of the world had crashed in on the little girl from Whitt Settlement, Pound, Virginia.

Delsie never recorded how she told sons Delmar and Virgil that she was giving them away to be raised by the home. Some of the Masons had talked to Virgil and told him about the home, and he began to tell his mother that he wanted to go live there. After all, he said, it was a better place than this old valley. Delmar's opinion on the matter wasn't kept in the family memories. Delsie did recount how she told her youngest daughter, Carrie Lee. Delsie asked her daughter to accompany her to the family garden. When they got there, instead of tending to the garden, Delsie took her little girl and said that they needed to have a serious talk. "Would you mind if Mother took you to a place to live and then left without taking you with her?" According to Delsie, Carrie Lee said that it would be okay with her. No father and now no family. But it was supposed to be a better place.

The local Masons came again to see Delsie. They told her again that she needed to sign the papers to give her children away to the Masonic Home in Richmond. "This is for the best," the men assured Delsie.

Laura, the oldest daughter, still at home and planning her wedding, wept and said that it was a horrible decision and that they were all mean to want to take away her brothers and sisters. Laura begged her mother, "Don't do this, please."

The papers were laid out, and Delsie signed them. Virgil Dotson, Delmar Dotson, Carrie Lee Dotson, and Ralph Dotson were now wards of the Masonic Home of Richmond, Virginia. The children were to be transported as soon as practicable to their new home and school. The Masonic Home for children had everything they needed from clothes to school supplies. And, after all, they could still come home for three weeks every summer. Virgil and Delmar would leave immediately, and Carrie Lee and Ralph would follow. The 1930 census taker recorded Delmar as a resident of the Masonic Home and under "Relationship to Head of Household" listed him as "inmate."

Chapter Two:

A STRANGE PLACE—THE MASONIC HOME OF VIRGINIA

I was torn from my family and set down in a strange place.... From the time I started my journey from Ringgold, Virginia, to the Masonic Home of Virginia, east of Richmond, I have virtually no memory of who delivered me to a strange place I would come to call Home. I don't even remember being united with my two older brothers, who had come to the Home a year before me. Nor can any image be evoked of a single adult I may have met on that fateful day." Excerpt from James Elwood Conner, *More Past Than Future.*[10]

The Masonic Home of Virginia, 1923 and 2015

The Masonic Lodge members of the Richmond, Virginia, area had discussed the problem for years. A place was desperately needed to care for the orphans of the area. The need for an orphanage was more pressing when one thought of the children of deceased former members of the Ancient Order going without proper care. Dr. George Potts, born in England and now a member of Astrea Lodge number 85, championed the cause of the orphans, especially of Masonic families, until action was finally proposed. A charter was sought in 1890 to establish a residence for needy children of Masonic Lodge members. Originally entitled the Masonic Orphan Asylum, the orphanage received a gift in 1890 of forty-four acres of farmland with living accommodations and "outbuildings" (barns, etc.). Supported by Masons around the State of Virginia, eventually over eight hundred children would be raised there.[11]

THE MASONS TALKED ME INTO IT

The Masons came time after time to talk Delsie into giving up the children. She finally agreed to give up the four youngest of her children, and she took them to the home in September of 1927. Concerned about her children growing up fatherless and believing that desperate measures were called for, she stated years later:

> When I decided . . . well I couldn't tell all the bad things that happened at Mill Creek. Two chillerns that never had a spankin'. Ralph and Carrie Lee. The railroad man asked how I raised such good children. He would let them ride free. We went to a place called Pikeville, Kentucky, to see [daughter] Laura. Doc Givens come to talk to me [about the children going to Richmond]. We had a garden way up in the holler. I talked to Carrie Lee there. "Would you cry if Mother was to take you to the Masonic Home and were to come back and leave you there?" Ralph didn't realize what it meant. "Every three months Mother will come to see you." She nodded her head that it would be all right. I went to Curry's Store and took them to Wise and spent the night. Mr. Lipscomb came and talked to us and said we would be so proud of these children. I couldn't breathe. They came at six a.m. to get us and we spent two days there [at the Home].[12]

The trip from the mountains of Southwest Virginia to the capital city of Richmond jarred Delsie to her core. The roads were rough, but the dread of leaving her children jostled her heart mile after mile. As they passed through valleys and into the flatlands of Virginia, it may have been the first time any of them had been out of the mountains. Delmar and Virgil went first to the orphanage, with Carrie Lee and Ralph to follow when they were a little older.

THE YEAR 1927

The records of the Masonic Home of Richmond, Virginia, show that Delmar Dotson of Wise County, Virginia, was admitted on Thursday September 8, 1927.[13]

Though the date was unrecognized outside of the Dotson family, it was a shattering event in the life of young Delmar. The year since his father's death had devolved with maddening speed, and now he was left alone in a strange place with strange ways. What would have been in the headlines that September day occurred on the other side of the world. Newspaper reports stated that the Empire of Japan was on the march in China, although at the moment the Imperial Army of Japan was making a strategic withdrawal from the Shandong Province. In Delmar's eleven-year-old world, this event would have had no significance, but that would change.

Delmar Dotson

Organization and attention to detail marked Delmar's new life. Every facet of the daily schedule was a part of the greater whole. The children slept twelve to fifteen to a room. Once you were in high school, more private quarters were arranged. James Elwood Conner remembered

*Delmar Dotson, age
twelve. Masonic Home
of Virginia*

winter nights, listening to the sigh of the radiator and the mournful wail of the Southern Railroad's train whistle, all while lying in a bed of clean sheets under a warm blanket.[14] Everyone ate in the large dining room where no one was allowed to leave until they had cleaned their plate. Meals were regular and wholesome.

Delmar was thrilled to death when siblings Carrie Lee and Ralph finally arrived at the Masonic Home. "Oh, Mother, I'm so happy," he said. He immediately took sister Carrie Lee under his wing to show her around. Delsie was due to leave after the Sunday meal and return to Pound alone. She remembered that the meal in the cafeteria was wonderful, though she herself had no appetite. One of the matrons of the home, Mrs. Williams, patted Delsie on the back as if to say the children would be fine. Little Ralph had an ear of corn and was intent on eating every bit of it. Mr. Lipscomb, who had driven Delsie to Richmond, told her it was time to go. They walked slowly to the car, and as its door closed, Delsie recalled,

> A door to my life closed. I cried for hours, all the way to Christiansburg. When we got home to the mountains I felt that they and everyone in them had turned on me. They seemed to close in on me, the mother who had abandoned her children, who had left them with strangers in a strange place.

Old Wib Branham, Delsie's father, waited on his daughter to return and tried to console her. He asked her if Richmond was a pretty place, but, "I wouldn't let Daddy or anyone talk to me."

Laura, who never had a cross word for anyone, came a few days later and howled, "I hate every one of you. I hate every one of you, you are such mean people."

"I told her how hard this was on all of us, but she could not be consoled. I told her, 'My children will have good manners and an education. The matter has been decided,'" Delsie said.

Now that the four youngest Dotson children were in Richmond, they each found their way in their new lives. Friendships were made, and they absorbed the traditions of the home. The older residents would have told Delmar and his brothers and sister that if you said the word "rabbit" on the first day of the month, it would bring you good luck. Virgil struggled the most with his new surroundings, running away in what would become a pattern of escapes over the next few years.

The Dotson children had been reared in church, and religious instruction would continue under the watchful eye of the matrons of the home. All children were required to attend Sunday School and church services each Sunday. On Wednesday nights, the matrons led prayer meetings where the Lord's Prayer and assigned Scripture passages were recited from memory. Many of the Sunday preachers came from the nearby Presbyterian Seminary in Richmond.[15] Delmar's little sister, Carrie Lee, stated that the matrons of the home made her listen to the preachers, but she never "took to heart" all that they were saying.[16]

School began each day on the grounds of the home after the completion of the morning chores. The values of the institution left little time for play. From

Carrie Lee and Ralph Dotson leaving for the Masonic Home of Virginia. September 1930

Ralph Dotson 1931. Age six

clothes to school supplies, the Masons provided the children with the necessities of life. Delmar embraced his new life and soon developed a reputation as someone who would look out for the underdog or anyone being bullied. One meal, he went back into the cafeteria looking for his seven-year-old sister, Carrie Lee, who had remained behind. Delmar found her crying over the cold spinach on her plate with one of the matrons standing over her. Carrie Lee was told in no uncertain terms that she would not leave the dining area until her plate was completely clean. Delmar walked up, scooped the spinach in his hand, put it on an empty plate nearby, and turned to the matron and said, "Now it's gone."

Carrie Lee with her protector and big brother, Delmar

The matron said nothing, and Carrie Lee got up to go with her brother. Carrie Lee recalled that the matrons loved Delmar and that he could get away with things like that.[17] Even though he was older she always knew that if she called, her brother Delmar would be there for her.

To keep the school going, many of the Lodges of Virginia contributed financial support and other things as well. The Lodge in Alexandria, Virginia, decided to donate twenty band instruments to the home. The thought was that a band made up of the children would be a great way to promote the home and encourage people to support the work. When the call went out for volunteers, Delmar signed up for the trumpet. He may have remembered his dad's musical ability and love for violin playing. Back in Pound, the Dotsons had a reputation of being fine musicians who could play by ear. Though sister Carrie Lee remembered Delmar's trumpet playing as "more enthusiastic than talented," he worked hard and travelled with the band to their various concerts under the leadership of the band director, G. Burton Mountcastle.[18] The band traversed the state of Virginia, performing concerts and promoting the work of the Masonic Home of Virginia.

This was something entirely new for Delmar. He fell in love with the trumpet and playing before the crowds of people. The trumpet was now ingrained as his instrument (though in later life Delmar would add the ukulele to his repertoire).

Delmar, front row at right, with his trumpet. Presumably,
Director Mountcastle is back row center

Finding his feet at the home, Delmar developed other interests as well. He was popular with his fellow students (Carrie Lee would add years later that he was "popular and proud"). Margaret Lemons, adopted into the home in 1928, and Delmar would develop more than a friendship over the next few years. Saturday nights were movie nights at the home, and Hollywood movies such as *All Quiet on the Western Front*

Delmar (back row second from left) and
Margaret (back row second from right) laugh
with their fellow students. October 1935

39

and *The Great Ziegfeld* appeared on the big screen to the delight of Delmar, Margaret, and their classmates.[19]

Margaret Lemons and Delmar Dotson

FERITE PRIMO. FERITE HUMILE. FERITE OMMINO.

The pride and joy of the Masonic Home and its supporters in the 1930s was its dominating football team. Eighty years later, employees of the home (no longer an orphanage but still in operation) would relate tales of football glory. In the middle of this was, of course, Delmar Dotson, who was to meet one of the most influential men of his life.

Pop "Bulldog" Turner represented both father and coach to his football players. Those boys able to make the cut were expected to give their very best on the gridiron. Coach Turner constantly reminded his boys that they represented the home with the way they played on the field.

Football in the 1930s was a game of conditioning. Substitutions were restricted, so players had to play both

Coach Pop "Bulldog" Turner (left) August 1937

offense and defense. The forward pass was not as popular as in modern football, and the run-oriented single-wing formation was the mainstay of most teams. With the success of the pro Chicago Bears, innovations like the "T formation" would come into vogue, but it was not yet the rage it would become. In the single-wing offense, the football was usually hiked to the tailback or fullback, and the offense tried to get two blockers on one defender, a double team. Since most teams ran the same offense, every coach needed an edge, an advantage to lead his team to victory, and Coach Turner believed he had a system that would do just that.

The Masonic Home Tomcats had three keys to lead them to victory, according to "Bulldog" Turner. Hit first. Hit low. Hit clean. The coach repeated the mantra over and over and delighted in stating his credo in Latin, "Ferite primo. Ferite humile. Ferite ommino." When asked about his secret formula for success, Coach Turner would also say with a wink that his boys were in excellent condition; "they have to walk everywhere."[20]

In later years when he would reflect on his coaching methods, he told a reporter, "I always have my boys begging for a good scrimmage, but I do not let them scrimmage over once a week." He added, "I think too much rough work makes the boys get stale. I always insist that they tackle hard and deadly while in a game." Bulldog Turner's view was if you tackled hard and hit the runner right, you would never get hurt "unless you have brittle bones."[21]

THE 1933 SEASON

The 1933 season did nothing but garner attention for this group of orphans who wanted to take on the local football elites. Delmar played in the backfield on a team where the average weight was 145 pounds, linemen included. Only the loss to the Oxford Masonic Home of North Carolina marred a dominating and perfect season.

vs. Oakwood 32–0
vs. Boy's Rome 45–0
vs. Sandston 26–0
vs. Fork Union Military Academy 13–12

vs. Patten Trade School, Elizabeth, PA 13–6
vs. CCC of Dillwyn, VA 12–0
vs. Southside KC 6–0
vs. Oxford (NC) Masonic Home 0–26
Record: 7–1[22]

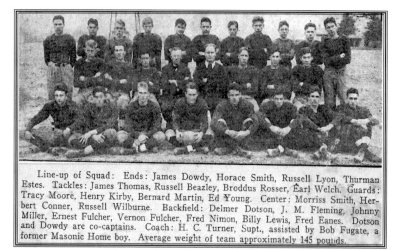

Line-up of Squad: Ends: James Dowdy, Horace Smith, Russell Lyon, Thurman Estes. Tackles: James Thomas, Russell Beazley, Broddus Rosser, Earl Welch. Guards: Tracy Moore, Henry Kirby, Bernard Martin, Ed Young. Center: Morriss Smith, Herbert Conner, Russell Wilburne. Backfield: Delmer Dotson, J. M. Fleming, Johnny Miller, Ernest Fulcher, Vernon Fulcher, Fred Nimon, Billy Lewis, Fred Eanes. Dotson and Dowdy are co-captains. Coach: H. C. Turner, Supt., assisted by Bob Fugate, a former Masonic Home boy. Average weight of team approximately 145 pounds.

Masonic Home Tomcats. Delmar is front and center holding the football.

THE SUMMER OF 1934

Summers were pleasant times of breaking from school and other warm weather activities. The boys would swim at a creek that they had dammed up in the Big Woods. When a polio epidemic spread in the nearby area, Coach Turner (also the school superintendent) had the boys destroy the dam and restricted the boys' visits outside.[23] Many of the boys would visit their families for up to three weeks in the summer. The Masons would even provide transportation for the families that needed it.

One special event came in the summer of 1934. To celebrate the work of the home, Monday, June 25, was set aside by the state lodges as "Masonic Home Day." The turnout was expected to be in the thousands and featured a tour of the grounds, a picnic, and a concert by the band.[24] Delmar would have enjoyed playing trumpet for the enthusiastic crowds of loyal supporters.

Typically Delmar enjoyed the time back home in Pound with his extended family. His older brothers had their own lives by now, but they still liked having Delmar around. Delmar's older brother Willie loaned Delmar his car and said all he needed was for Delmar to give him a ride home when his shift was over at the coal mines. What was supposed to be a simple ride turned into much more when other family members wanted to come along for a ride. Delsie, no doubt cherishing every moment with her son at home, hopped in, and soon enough Delmar's brother Virgil decided to join in as well. Despite his early enthusiasm, Virgil never took to the Masonic Home, and after running away several times, he finally returned to the Pound. On this day, he had an ulterior motive for coming along; he desperately wanted to drive the car. Virgil's car-driving skills, or lack thereof, must have been known to the family. Willie had instructed Delmar that under no circumstances could he let his brother Virgil take the wheel. Delmar, however, gave in to Virgil's pleading and soon they were off. The car was too much for Virgil to handle, and it soon careened off the narrow road on the way to the coal mine. The resulting crash of the automobile nearly killed Delsie and put all of them in the hospital. However, when she found out that that hospital charged $7.00 a day, she recovered quickly. Virgil suffered a fractured skull and eventually had a metal plate installed in his head. Delmar got off the lightest but had both sides of his jaw broken, and they had to wire his mouth shut so that the fractures could heal.[25] The Masonic Home sent a car for Delmar, and his time at home ended.[26] (Some family sources state that this wreck happened in 1936 and not 1934.)

Delsie crying as Ralph returns to the Masonic Home

The 1934 Season

"Masonic Home Swamps South Hill High 87–0" beamed the headline in the *Richmond Times-Dispatch*. The newspaper was finally paying attention.

"Distributing the scoring among nine players, Masonic Home gridders, playing on a slippery field of mud, with the ease of hockey players on rinks, overwhelmed South Hill High 87–0, yesterday afternoon on the Masonic Home field. Captain Gerald Fleming personally accounted for three touchdowns and booted two placements. Jay Miller, left half, scored six touchdowns, Farley scored two, Eanes, Burdette, Faulkner had one apiece, while Dowdy, Nelson, and Smith scored one extra point each. Miller's 45-yard dash in the first period and 50-yard sprint in the third were the outstanding runs. Both resulted in scores. Burdette's touchdown and conversion where the only points scored on passes."[27]

In the win over Culpepper, the *Times-Dispatch* mentioned Delmar coming in as a substitute in the crushing victory.[28]

> vs. Miller Manual School, Crozet 6–0
> vs. Fork Union Military Academy 0–0
> vs. Sandston A.C. 29–0
> vs. Culpepper High 18–0
> vs. South Hill High 87–0
> vs. Culpepper High 25–0
> vs. Patton Trade School 26–7
> vs. Oxford (North Car) Masonic Home 15–0

The Tomcats even avenged the previous season's only loss by defeating the Masonic Home of North Carolina 15–0. Coach Turner's undefeated season was blemished only by a draw versus the Fork Union Military Academy early in the season. On top of everything else, the boys outscored their opponents 206 to 7.

The 1935 Season

As Delmar and the boys from the orphanage continued to win, they garnered more and more attention for their powerhouse football team and the school. The *Richmond Times-Dispatch* reported that the school "cares for 250 boys and girls from 6 to 18 years of age, and is the outstanding philanthropic work of Masons in the State."[29] The team overwhelmed, outran, and outhit their opponents on their way to another stellar season.

vs. Arrow Juniors 26–0
vs. Culpepper High 56–0
vs. Hampton-Sydney Freshmen 6–6
vs. Westhampton High 19–0
vs. George Washington, Alexandria, VA 7–19
vs. South Hill 39–0
vs. Ashland High 19-0
vs. Fredericksburg High 26–14
6–1–1 record and outscored opponents 198–39

Hosts In Thanksgiving Morning Game Here

This is the football squad of the Masonic Home, which will play Camp Chesapeake here tomorrow morning at 10:30 o'clock, on the Masonic Home grounds. The Gloucester eleven defeated Benedictine, but lost to McGuire's. In the picture, left to right, are: Bottom row—Clarke, U. Humphries, B. Humphries, Birch, Smith, Bennett, Captain Fugate, Davis. Middle—Blackburn, Nelson, Sawyers, Robinson, Buchanan, Hager, Matheny, Moschler, Dotson. Top—Coach Turner, Dowdy, Dozier, Felton, Wright (manager), Cundiff, Craig, Morse, Marks, Assistant Coach Eugene Cook, University of Richmond. [News Leader photo by Dement]

Delmar is second row far right

Delmar is in the second row, far left

THE SPRING OF 1936

Though most of the students left the Masonic Home by the age of eighteen, Delmar was almost nineteen years old by the spring of 1936, and he seriously thought about his future. His sister Carrie Lee remembered that Delmar decided that Hollywood was the place for him; he took his savings and headed west. The adventurous Dotson eventually appeared as an extra in several "B" westerns (the names were forgotten), but Delmar sent back photos of his short-lived stardom. Not bad for a poor boy from the mountains of Virginia.

Delmar Dotson April 1936

*Deadeye Delmar
Dotson April 1936*

THE 1936 SEASON

The fall of 1936 saw the football team continue its dominance, and by 1937 Masonic Home officials would be lobbying around the state of Virginia for their team to play in the Little Tobacco Bowl Game, sponsored by the American Legion.[30] When sportswriter Tom Wiley of the *Richmond Times-Dispatch* asked Coach Turner to name the best player he coached, he named fullback John Cundiff. Other boys he picked as his best players ever were Ural Humphries, J. C. Matheny, James Thomas, Delmar Dotson, and Morris Smith. Thomas, Dotson, and Smith were members of the 1936 team, which, Turner proudly recalled, was undefeated and unscored upon. They only weighed an average of 144 pounds, and one back only weighed 138 pounds. The captain of the undefeated 1936 team was Delmar Dotson, son of Albert and Delsie of Pound, Virginia.[31]

vs. Hargrave Military Academy 7–0
vs. George Washington, Alexandria, VA 6–0
vs. Victoria High 31–0
vs. National Training School 19–0
vs. Hampton-Sydney Freshman 0–0
vs. Patten Trade School 18–0
A 5–0–1 record and outscored opponents 81–0

MAY 3, 1937

Graduating from high school at the Masonic Home of Virginia, Delmar was discharged on May 3, 1937. He was twenty-one years of age and was the 467th child admitted to the home. On this date, actress Jean Harlow was on the cover of *Life* magazine. Mrs. Wallace Simpson was granted a divorce and could now marry England's Edward VIII. The dirigible LZ 129 Hindenburg left for America and was due to dock in New Jersey in three fateful days. Margaret Mitchell was awarded the Pulitzer Prize for her novel *Gone with the Wind.* And last but not least, Delmar Dotson moved back home to Pound, Virginia.

The next steps for Delmar Dotson were lost to the family memory. There were a few vague ideas and recollections, but time and distance separated him from the collective family memory. Delmar's steps were largely unknown until one photograph revealed his secret.

Delmar back at home on
Mill Creek, Pound, VA, 1937

Chapter Three:

FROM HERE TO HAWAII

THE MYSTERY

June 27, 2013

Aloha Michael:

That is a nice photo. The inscription reads: "Kapiolani Park." Before I noticed that, I was already certain that it was the old Kapiolani Park Bandstand. I

Delmar Dotson on trumpet, second from left

could even see some of the ironwood trees in the distance. And of course the unmistakable construction of the old open air bandstand. In September 1939, my father, Harry B. Soria, Sr., was the remote broadcast manager for the largest of the 2 radio stations in Hawaii at that time, KGU. It is very possible that he was broadcasting this event but I don't see any microphones in the photo area. There may have been one out front. This is primarily a shot of his buddies in the brass section. I do notice that, as was the case back then, all of the brass section appear to be Caucasian, while other members of the band, especially the rhythm section, appear to be local Hawaii ethnic.

I know that the Royal Hawaiian Band played there regularly, but their uniforms were more elaborate and all white. This appears to be a very large orchestra, so it could have been representing a ship, or an organization, etc. Almost looks like an all-star band. For example, I could be wrong, but it almost looks like 2 back to back pianos. And none of the musicians stand out to me as guys that I have followed the careers of in Hawaiian music. I really looked closely at "Johnny" the guitarist with the glasses, as he looks like a local guy. But I'm coming up empty on a name match. Wish I could be of more help to you. You say that he was killed in the war. This may possibly have been related to where he was working?

All the best,

Harry B.
Harry B. Soria, Jr.
Territorial Airwaves
Hear Territorial Airwaves shows at: www.territorialairwaves.com
Your Source for the History of Hawaiian Music[32]

That Delmar Dotson had found his way to Hawaii was certain. That he played in a band or bands was also certain. In the family memory, Delmar had joined the army, but the rest was lost to time.[33] Further complicating matters is the paucity of records from this period of time.[34]

In his twenty-first year of age, Delmar now stood on his own, no longer an orphan but a man expected to make his way in the world. The Masonic Home had provided him an education and a father figure in Coach Turner. Delmar knew how to captain a football team, could play the trumpet, and he knew the value of hard work. However, the nation was in the midst of the Great Depression, and jobs were hard to come by, even in the coal mines of the mountains back home in Pound, Virginia.

The circumstances of his move from Virginia to Hawaii and the specifics of what he did there remain matters of speculation, but for those who knew Delmar at the time, no one seemed to be surprised that he would travel to an exotic location and play trumpet professionally.

The details of Delmar's true past began to surface when a distant relative brought forth an unusual picture, claimed to be the long-since departed Delmar Dotson. In the picture of Delmar with his trumpet, the unusual, almost Russian-looking uniform proved to be the decisive key. The uniform is khaki with the regulation tie and the stripes of a private in the military. The hat is a large shako with the golden image of a wolf emblazoned on the front. Crossed ammo belts and boots complete the ensemble. The uniform could only belong to one unit in the annals of the United States Army. Delmar had enlisted in the 27th Infantry Regiment, nicknamed "The Wolfhounds." The 27th Regiment was headquartered in Schofield Barracks, Oahu, The Hawaiian Islands.

Private Delmar Dotson, 27th Infantry Regiment, Schofield Barracks, The Hawaiians

NEC ASPERA TERRENT "UNDAUNTED"

Below him under the blows of the February Hawaiian sun the quadrangle gasped defenselessly, like an exhausted fighter. Through the heat haze and the thin mid-morning film of the parched red dust came up a muted orchestra of sounds.

Pvt. Robert E. Lee Prewitt meets G Company in James Jones' *From Here to Eternity.*[35]

A unique glimpse of life in the prewar army comes from author James Jones, who wrote a fictionalized account of the time he served in the prewar 27th Infantry Regiment. Jones had served in "E" Company, the "boxing company" of the 27th, and his thinly disguised revelations of the peacetime army made up contents of his novel *From Here to Eternity*. The real 27th Regiment was only a few decades old in the 1930s, young by army standards, but had already garnered an illustrious reputation.

After the completion of the Spanish-American War, the 1898 Treaty of Paris granted the United States of America control of the Philippine Islands and also gave America an interest in the Pacific. Once it became clear that President McKinley would not free the Philippines, guerilla warfare erupted. The 27th Infantry Regiment was formed to put down this revolution. The headquarters, band, and first battalion sailed in January 1902. Fighting Moro Muslims in the southern island of Mindanao alongside Captain John J. Pershing (later to command all American forces in Europe in World War One) won the regiment the congratulations of President Teddy Roosevelt.

In 1918, at the conclusion of World War I, the 27th Regiment was sent to the Russian province of Vladivostok to join the Siberian Expeditionary Forces. The regiment fought alongside the army of Japan against the Russian Bolsheviks (followers of Vladimir Lenin). Japanese General Otani took note of the regiment's ability to rapidly pursue the forces of the Bolsheviks and keep them off balance. The Bolsheviks, chased so rapidly, compared the American soldiers to Russian Wolfhounds, who were known for their speed and tenacity. The name was gladly adopted by the soldiers of the twenty-seventh and became the regimental nickname, which is still in use today.[36]

Sergeant Major Clyde Fisel, who had joined the regiment in 1912, reminisced years later of his time in the 27th. Most of his memories of Siberian Russia were not of the pursuit of the Communists but the severe food shortages, the rain, and the ever-present Russian mud. Finally, he recalled the snow and ice when the mercury dropped out of the bottom of the thermometer.[37] Fisel would not be the last soldier on Russian soil to bemoan the mud and snow of a Russian winter.

In 1921, the 27th Regiment received orders to occupy Schofield Barracks and Fort Shafter, Oahu, the Hawaiian Islands, as its permanent home station. The regiment made up a part of the newly formed Hawaiian Division. The Hawaiian Division held the distinction for years of being one of only three Army Divisions not identified by a number (the others were the Philippine Division and the Americal Division). Fifteen years later, Private Delmar Dotson reported for duty as a soldier and a trumpet player in the United States Army, 27th Infantry Regiment, Band Company. By 1938, fourteen thousand army personnel, approximately 10 percent of the army's forces at the time, were stationed in Hawaii.[38]

Shoulder Sleeve Insignia of the Hawaiian Division. Later deactivated and replaced by the 25th Division in October 1941.

AN ARMY MUSICIAN

Music had played an important role in the army since 1775 when a Fife and Drum Corps played to celebrate the victory of Ethan Allen and the Green Mountain Boys at Fort Ticonderoga.[39] While in France during World War I, General Pershing heard the excellent quality of the military bands of England and France, and after the war, he placed a renewed emphasis on music in the army. In Delmar's day, even the bandmaster was European. Warrant Officer Chura had been born in Bohemia of the old Austro-Hungarian Empire.

The 27th Infantry Regiment took great pride in their band and decided to use the Russian style of Cossack dress for the marching uniforms. The distinctive look would make them stand out from any other unit in the US Army. The regiment even adopted a mascot to accompany the band when marching in parade. The dog was a Russian Borzoi with the pretentious name of Aleksandr Woronoza Kolchak, registered with the American Kennel Club. During Delmar's time in the regiment, the dog was known as Kolchak II.[40]

Peacetime army days were made up of routines and schedules. For an active band, marching practice was as essential as instrumental practice. After all, you never knew who might drop in. Schofield Barracks had been established in 1908, and the Army Post consisted of a number of

27th Infantry Regimental Band. Delmar is in the back middle of the picture.

Delmar's bandmate: Trumpeter Burns

Fellow trumpeters PFC Beltz and Pvt. Parella

quadrangle-style structures, or "quads." The post had been named after a Union general from the American Civil War and included such amenities as a library, bowling alley, gymnasium, boxing arena, and post theater.[41] Visitors from the mainland made the boat ride to come and see the tropical paradise and its resident army units, sometimes called the "Pineapple Army."

The beautiful island of Oahu served as a serene setting as Delmar adjusted to life in the Pacific. Gone were the winters of Virginia, but new sights and sounds awaited him. Some of the local shops even catered to individual regiments. If he needed a tailor, a shop in town specialized in serving the men of the famed 27th. Leisure time allowed for seeing the sights, both geographical and feminine, and for playing in various pick-up bands. This was the height of the Big Band era, and the tunes of Glenn Miller, Tommy Dorsey, Bennie Goodman, and so many others were the rage. Delmar began dating a girl during his off-duty time and even sent a picture to his sister Carrie Lee for

Delmar and his girl in Hilo, The Hawaiians. His note said she was Portuguese.

The 27th Infantry Regiment Band on the march

27th Regiment Dance Band. The logo on the bandstands is that of the Hawaiian Division.

Downtown Honolulu, the Hawaiians, circa 1930s

approval. He noted on the back of the picture, "This was taken in Hilo, Hawaii. She is Portuguese. Nice, yes."

Having already experienced dramatic change with his time in the orphanage, when put into a new situation, Delmar quickly made friends, mostly fellow band members. The numerous parades and reviews kept them busy, but the weekends were free to play with local musicians in the various clubs and parks. The army is nothing without gossip, and soon the rumors were flying that the band was going to accompany a very special guest singer. Practices must have intensified, and everyone would have tried to guess who the mystery soloist could be.

I'LL HAVE A SHIRLEY TEMPLE, PLEASE

Too young to drink, international movie star Shirley Temple sat at the bar in the Royal Hawaiian Hotel (she liked the hotel because of its pink color). The staff at the Mai Tai Bar told her they would create a drink just for her, so they mixed ginger ale, grenadine, a splash of orange juice, and a cherry. The "Shirley Temple" was born.

Known as "America's Sweetheart," Miss Temple visited Hawaii numerous times including 1937 and 1939. The 1939 visit especially focused on the troops, and this was most likely when she was accompanied by trumpeter Delmar Dotson and the 27th Regimental Band. Though the press always declared that everyone "adored" her, apparently some members of the band, seeing her away from the crowds, had a slightly different opinion of her. The troubles of the child star.[42]

Once things returned to normal, Delmar and the band moved back into their routine. World events were moving in a worrisome direction. Japan was on the march in China, and the Nazi Party was rapidly rearming the German people. However, in 1939 America, even in the American Territories, those events were a world away.

Shirley Temple wearing the hat of the 27th Infantry Regiment Band

Concerts continued for Delmar and friends, and a favorite place was the Kapiolani Park, home of the Kodak Hula Show. Kapiolani Regional Park was the largest and oldest public park in Hawaii, located in Honolulu near Waikiki, just beyond Kuhio Beach Park and

the Waikiki residential neighborhood. The Shell was an open-air place for bands to perform. It was regularly used for concerts by, most famously, the Royal Hawaiian Band. Delmar and friends played with civilian bands in the area, and Delmar even began to moonlight as a singer on KGU radio. One picture he sent home to his family included a note from Delmar, written in the family hand: "Where I work when I'm singing to millions of people. HA HA." According to music historian Harry B. Soria Jr., this photo (next page top right) was taken on the roof of the three-story Honolulu Advertiser Building, which was a popular place for publicity photos. The newspaper occupied the first two floors and allowed their radio station to occupy the third (top) floor of the building. The antenna was on the roof of the building. Years later the building would be used to film the television show *Hawaii 5-0*.[43]

*Honolulu Advertiser
Building 1929*

*Crooner Delmar at the studios
of the KGU radio station*

On top of everything else, Delmar was promoted to corporal and declared himself, "US Army's best Non-Commissioned Officer." A close inspection of the photo shows that his hat bears the harp insignia of a US Army musician.

The years passed, and with his army enlistment almost up, Delmar faced the dilemma of so many soldiers—whether to reenlist or not. He had found a home in the army, at least as much a home as he had had at the orphanage. But the struggles of routine in the peacetime army made him wonder whether another enlistment was what he wanted. In one of his final army photos in Hawaii, he strikes a fighting stance for the family

*Corporal Dotson,
ready to fight*

back home. No word exists on whether he had been with the boxing men of Company E or the yet undiscovered James Jones. Ironically, the combative pose evokes the next and tragic years of the life of Delmar Dotson of Pound, Virginia.

Chapter Four:

RETURN TO SERVICE

Delmar, Laura Dotson Spradlin, Carrie Lee, Ralph. Late 1930s. History of the Pound, vol. 3, p. 140 says this picture is circa 1937

For the first time since childhood, Delmar had returned to live in the mountains of Southwest Virginia. Leaving the army shortly after April 1940 (the 1940 census lists "Corporal Datson"[sic] as being at Schofield Barracks in April), he had returned to The Pound after an absence of over a decade. Most of his brothers and sisters had their own families and had moved on. Lola and Laura were married. Glenn was away in the army, never seeming to do much to care for the family situation. Willie was married, and Virgil had never been quite the same since the car accident. Carrie Lee and Ralph were still at the Masonic Home. Even Delsie had a new family. In overwhelming distress, oldest daughter, Lola, had brought her four children and ran off and left them with Delsie to rear. With Delsie occupied with another brood to raise (while two of her own children were still in the Masonic Home), Delmar moved back and sought to find his place as he looked for work.

Delmar and a girlfriend

Rena Dotson, Delmar's sister-in-law, remembered Delmar having helped her and brother Willie move into a new house. Rena was expecting a child, and as soon as she was in her new home, she propped up her feet and declared that she needed to rest. Delmar told her not to worry; he would clean up her yard for her. Sizing up the yard and thinking that this yard would be a source of ongoing work, he borrowed a hoe and dug up all the grass in the yard and piled it up to one side. No more yard work! When the shock registered that the green yard was now dirt, Delmar told Rena and Willie, "This way you'll not have to cut the grass or care for it." Delmar would show up at Rena's door whenever she had fresh milk and cornbread. After consuming the entire skillet, he would remark, "Don't tell Mother, but your bread is so much better than hers." Neighbors noticed Delmar's upbeat and relaxed attitude as spring turned to summer. He had a penchant for baggy clothes and floppy hats. Those who noticed his lack of a job knew that that couldn't continue.

Delmar back in Pound, Virginia, sporting his army campaign hat

In Rena's opinion, Delsie talked Delmar into returning to the service. Delsie may have needed the finances, or it may have been that, so long removed, the mountains no longer truly felt like home. Delmar had walked away from the army as a non-commissioned officer, but when the choice came to reenlist, he chose a different path this time. The grass never grew under Delmar Dotson's feet. Rena remembered Delmar stating, "Mother wants me to go back into the service and things are getting rough over there. I'm not mad at anyone and don't want to go." On the way to the recruiting station, Delmar stopped in to tell Rena good-bye, saying, "Mother won't let me have any peace. She wants her checks to start back coming in."[44] Delmar's reticence to go to war reflected the mood of much of the nation. Difficult to understand in light of the modern "American Century," the United States' self-image was not one of world policeman. Despite the best efforts of British leadership, President Franklin D. Roosevelt faced intense political pressure at home to keep America out of another European conflict.

Delsie got her wish for Delmar to return to the service, and she received this postcard in the mail in the summer of 1940:

Richmond Recruiting District
United States Army
Richmond, Virginia
June 15, 1940

Your son Delmar was enlisted in the Regular Army this date for Air Corps. He left Richmond today for Langley Field, Virginia, feeling very happy that he had enlisted. Before leaving he was advised to write home to his parents after he gets settled in the Army and I believe he will. If you desire to write him, address your letter as follows: Private Delmar Dotson, Air Corps, Langley Field, Virginia

Very Truly Yours,

Joseph L. O'Brien
Acting Recruiting Officer

LANGLEY FIELD

On March 1, 1935, Langley Field became the center of tactical aviation for the United States Army. On that day the Army Air Corps underwent a major reorganization, which created the General Headquarters Air Force, commonly referred to as GHQ AF.[45] The 2nd Bombardment Group was headquartered at Langley Field, and on March 1, 1937, became the first tactical unit to possess the Boeing B-17 Bomber. This plane, massive for its time, was nicknamed the "Flying Fortress." On his arrival, Delmar must have been impressed with the four-engine behemoths on the runway and in the hangers.

Delmar's arrival at Langley also coincided with a dramatic change in the operating tempo of the airbase. Germany's invasion of Poland had instigated a war in Europe, and America, though neutral in national policy, was rapidly increasing its own military spending as well as selling armaments to England, France, and China. The training focus of Langley Field was on long-distance aerial navigation. The Martin B-10 and Boeing B-17 Bombers were pushed to their limits, and the navigational acumen of the men was tested as well. Whether on overland flights or Goodwill Missions to other countries, the men were preparing for war and they knew it. Langley Field airmen such as Lt. Curtis LeMay were learning lessons they would use in the coming conflict. Seven years later, Gen. Curtis LeMay would become a name synonymous with long-range heavy bombing as he oversaw the utter devastation of the home islands of Japan.

The Langley Airbase population continued to grow from the 1935 numbers of 160 officers and 1,387 enlisted men to the February 1940 numbers of a total of 5,849 personnel. The large number of new recruits meant that many new airmen had to wear their civilian clothes, as shortages of all kinds plagued the readiness efforts of the military. One Langley observer noted in 1940, "It was not uncommon to see a detachment of recruits at drill wearing a mixture of coveralls, blue denim, khaki, woolen olive drab, and civilian clothing, some with and some without overcoats."[46] Delmar would have lived in hastily constructed enlisted men's quarters, a far cry from the Quads of Schofield Barracks, The Hawaiians.[47]

For the rest of his short career, Delmar would wear the shoulder patch of the GHQ AF on his dress uniforms.

The fact that Delmar remained at Langley into 1941 as the Air Corp constantly expanded and reorganized meant that he was either assigned to the 2nd Bombardment Group (most likely) or to one of the Air Corps headquarters units stationed there. Some of Delmar's military records began to appear at this time, and at his appointment to Langley Field on June 15, 1940, he stood 5 feet 9½ inches and weighed 150 pounds. He

Dotson's shoulder patch
GHQ AF

probably weighed close to his playing weight back in his Tomcat football days. He is recorded as having blue eyes and brown hair. An ongoing mystery revolves around his date of birth. His Air Corps records show that he was born June 15, 1918, and not 1916 as was true. Family tradition says that he wanted to be a pilot when he signed up for the Air Corp, and since pilot training had an age limit, he may have changed his birth year so that he would be eligible. Possibly, Delmar tried to join the Air Corp as a pilot in 1937, and after washing out of pilot training, joined the 27th to play in their band. Regardless of the circumstances when he arrived at Langley Field, he was once again in the enlisted ranks.

Langley Airfield may have suffered from a shortage of supplies but not from a shortage of visitors. President Franklin D. Roosevelt visited Langley during Delmar's time there on July 29, 1940. The Duke of Kent made an inspection in August of 1941.[48] In the midst of the chaos, new units were constantly being formed and then divided and made into additional units. The dual threats of the Far East and Europe meant that a two-front war was a theoretical possibility, regardless of the prevalent isolationism of much of the nation.

Cpl. Delmar Dotson Army Air Corp at Langley Field. He has his stripes back. Circa 1940

Picture from Delmar of Langley Airfield, Virginia, circa 1940. The parked planes may be Curtis P-36s and Martin B-10 Bombers and the plane on the runway a C-47.

THE 43RD BOMBARDMENT GROUP

This 43rd Bombardment Group (Heavy) was activated at Langley Field January 15, 1941, and one of its charter members was Delmar Dotson, soon to make sergeant. Four months later, the Army Air Corp was renamed the Army Air Force on June 20, 1941. In addition to the birth of the 43rd, the 65th Squadron was also activated that January day. With the constant shifting of higher headquarters and the formation of a new unit, it would be some time before the group became fully operational. For experienced soldiers like Delmar, promotion came rapidly, along with opportunities for additional training.

CHANUTE FIELD, ILLINOIS

December 16, 1941 *The* (Zanesville, Ohio) *Times Recorder* Staff Sergeant Delmar Dotson who recently graduated from the air corps technical school at Chanute Field, Illinois spent part of his furlough here with Mr. and Mrs. James L. Wilson. He has been transferred to the municipal airport at Bangor, Maine.[49]

Delmar would list New Lexington, Ohio, as his home address for part of the war, presumably because his older sister Laura (now Spradlin) lived there with her family. Being selected to attend technical school was a reflection of Delmar's intellect and leadership ability. The new multiengine planes were becoming so complex that an expanded crew was needed for safe operation. In addition to the pilot and copilot, a flight engineer was a senior enlisted man whose job was to look at the gauges during takeoff and landing. He also doubled as the top turret machine gunner when not performing his engineering duties. With the air force becoming even more technologically driven, the technical school, commanded by Col. Gerald Brant, fueled the air force's need for large numbers of highly trained personnel.[50] The official Army Air Force description of Delmar's job was as follows:

AIRPLANE MECHANIC-GUNNER MOS 748: Aerial Engineer-Gunner

Assists pilot in operation of a multiple-engined airplane by maintaining a constant check on its mechanical functioning. Fires aerial guns in combat. Notes readings of engine and navigation instruments, reporting any indication of malfunctioning, and maintains log of engine performance. Makes limited repairs and mechanical adjustments while in flight. Transfers fuel from one tank to another as consumed, in such manner as to maintain balance of airplane, Assists pilot in deciding whether airplane should be grounded when serious malfunctioning develops, Reports needed repairs to maintenance crew.[51]

When Delmar started Air Force Technical School, America was planning for war, but when he graduated, America was at war. The bombing of Pearl Harbor would have had special significance to Delmar since he had spent so much time at Schofield Barracks and in Hawaii. The nation reeled from the shock of the attack, and a flurry of mobilization activity took place. A few days after Pearl Harbor, Adolf Hitler and Germany declared war on the United States, and another world war was at hand.

Carrie Lee Dotson headed for nursing school as she completed her time at the Masonic Home. She too would be headed for war, but not yet. On a day off from her studies at the Medical College of Virginia, she and some of her fellow nursing students were strolling along in downtown Richmond, Virginia. To her surprise, whom should she see but big brother Delmar and some of his buddies headed right for them!

Delmar's little sister Carrie Lee was surprised to see Delmar and some buddies walking down the sidewalk in Richmond, Virginia. Normally, Delmar had doted on her, but on this day, he seemed distracted and aloof. Carrie Lee thought maybe it was something about her that he didn't like; after all, she had grown up and was no longer the little girl he had protected at the orphanage. Even more unusual was Delmar's lack of attention to her female friends; he always wanted her to pick out a pretty nurse for a date. Maybe he didn't want his friends making passes at his kid sister. The image of him leaving would remain in her mind and in her dreams.

Two pictures Delmar sent home from Pearl Harbor sometime during the war

BANGOR AIRFIELD, MAINE

Relocating to the northeastern United States marked the first of many moves for the operations 43rd Bombardment Group. By August 28, 1941, the move was completed, and the unit resumed its full training schedule. The B-17s arrived in October, and the crews began familiarizing themselves with the complex airplane.[52] As the transfer of personnel and equipment allowed, the unit began flying antisubmarine patrols. Once the war began, German submarines began torpedoing boats right off the American coast. Air patrols were no longer exercises but real-world missions. Bangor Field, later renamed Dow Air Force Base, also served as a way station to ferry planes to England and Europe. Speculation was that the unit was headed to fight the Germans across the Atlantic. Yet Europe was not to be for the sons of the 43rd and Delmar. For Delmar and the others, this was also a time to learn their jobs and develop the aircraft teamwork vital for effective combat. Delmar could almost hear Coach Turner reminding the men to "hit first." The brutal Maine winter in no way foreshadowed the future of the 43rd. The snow-covered runways and frozen fingers would soon be distant memory, however.

THE DOTSONS GO TO WAR

When President Roosevelt declared war on the Empire of Japan and later Nazi Germany, the Dotson family prepared to enter the fight. Five of Delsie's children would soon be in uniform. Glenn was a career soldier (and a career ladies' man, if the family stories are half true) in the army. Delmar was in the Army Air Force. Soon little brother Ralph would be in the army, and even little sister Carrie Lee was destined to be an army nurse. Willie went into the army at the end of the war. Willie had served in the peacetime army but had been medically discharged after inhaling chemical munitions.

Sgt. Delmar Dotson young and brave with his enlisted aircrew wings and the National Defense Medal showing he was in federal service the year before the war began

John Branham, Vernon Branham, Delmar Dotson, and Willie Dotson with Old Wib Branham in front. Pound, Virginia

Captain Glenn Dotson

Pvt. Ralph Dotson, US Army

Pvt. Ralph Dotson goes to war. He is far left on the upper deck.

Lt. Carrie Lee Dotson, US Army Nursing Corps. She would be the third of Delsie's children to serve in the Pacific.

Another Dotson Goes to War picture

Another Dotson Goes to War picture

Another Dotson Goes to War picture

With the 43rd's work completed in the States, it was now time to deploy overseas. The abrupt start to the war and the vast beginning of the war had negated all the years of prewar strategic planning. Now the war needed American troops on almost every continent. The American military struggled to equip the hordes of new soldiers with the basic necessities of military life. Complicating this even further was the wide variety of climates and conditions now confronting combat units. From the Artic to the tropics, the logistical challenges would be overwhelming for the foreseeable future. As ill-equipped units struggled to hold off the Japanese Empire, green units prepared to invade Africa. The war was not going well, and some units needed to be sacrificed in

Delsie Dotson. Five-Star Mother (five children in the service). Worried.

order to buy time for new equipment to arrive and better tactics to take shape. The 43rd Bombardment Group was ordered to move, first to Boston, where the support troops would prepare to sail to their wartime assignment. Planes would be ferried by minimal crews to their destination. Once all of the men and equipment of the 43rd Bomb Group reunited at their destination, they would be introduced to their foe.

Chapter Five:

41-24552

#552

"I happened to be placed on Project 299 just about the time I planned to be married. We had the ceremony on Saturday; I took Sunday and Monday off." Edward Curtis Wells, YB-17 Project Engineer Boeing Aircraft 1934.[53]

They were like the prophets of the Old Testament, predicting the future. They said that someday the skies would be full of airplanes dropping bombs on enemy ships and armies, winning the battles on air power alone. At the end of World War I, this seemed like an impossibility due to the state of aviation technology. The engines and airframes would not allow for the massive air armadas that had been predicted. However, as airplane technology progressed in the years after World War I, the possibility of a large bomber that could outfly interceptor aircraft and drop large payloads of explosives on enemy targets became more and more a reality. The Great Depression meant miniscule budgets for development and acquisition, so the few prototypes of the ideal heavy bomber were often designed at the expense of the aircraft manufacturing companies and not the government. One such example was Boeing Aircraft Company's "Project 299."

The Boeing Aircraft Company believed that they could design a large airplane that would be the answer to the need for a bomber that could project strength and deliver destruction to any foe foolish enough to take on the United States. The world crisis and increased military spending promised an increased likelihood that the plane would be accepted by the Air Corps and that orders would be given to produce the massive four-engine bomber. Initial reports stated that the Project 299 plane was too much aircraft for one pilot, or even two, to handle. The standardized checklist, a list of preflight steps taken before a plane could take off, was developed to assist the pilot. The number of steps was considered too long to trust to memory. Years of difficult negotiations between company and government representatives finally culminated with the B-17 Bomber, one of the iconic machines of World War II.

She was born on the production line of Boeing's Seattle, Washington, production facility. Some poets describe flying machines as instruments of beauty or grace, with verbal pictures of soaring amidst the blue skies and touching the heavens with wings. This plane, #552, was built for a different purpose; she was intended to be an instrument of death and destruction. For centuries blacksmiths and craftsmen had designed and built instruments of war and destruction, and she was only latest in a long line of suits of armor. The aluminum skin was laden with some of the best technology of the day.

Number 552 was American made in almost every sense of the word. The raw materials were largely mined in America and the ore refined by Americans into the materials the American craftsmen would need. With the possible exception of the rubber parts, the aluminum and steel came from American mines to American factories until, finally, the components reached the Boeing Aircraft Company in Seattle, Washington. The windows and nose cone were made of polymethyl methacrylate, a thermoplastic commonly known as Plexiglas.

Over 103 feet from wing tip to wing tip, she was also seventy-four-feet long and almost two stories tall. Her rib cage consisted of a series of aluminum alloy rings that formed the fuselage, or center, of the plane. Her shoulders, the wing spars, supported four of the biggest engines of the day made by the Curtiss-Wright Company. When the Wright brothers first flew in 1903, their aluminum-cased engine produced 12 horsepower. Now the company bearing their name produced engines that could generate 1,200 horsepower in an air-cooled nine-cylinder arrangement. A turbo-supercharger on each engine gave a power boost for takeoffs and high-altitude flying.

Even with its warlike intentions, many pilots reportedly enjoyed flying the B-17. After the rituals of the preflight routine were completed and the B-17 picked up speed, this plane wanted to fly. When flown without its military payload, the plane floated from the runway into the air with a grace that belied the behemoth qualities of the plane. Though not without its idiosyncrasies, the B-17 was a forgiving airplane, and its ability to absorb damage and bring its crew home would become legendary; in fact, some of the survival stories would almost border on the miraculous.

The design for the B-17 was half a decade old, and by the time #552 was born, war modifications had significantly changed her appearance from that of her forbearers. From the original B-17s, named Model 299 through the Model D, the bombers were found to be lacking many essentials for modern warfare. The E model was the first to incorporate wartime lessons learned in Europe. Better engines and new turret systems complemented the improved wing root design that imparted strength and survivability to the aircraft.[54] Number 552 included the latest mass production improvements and even had a "computer" (somewhat resembling a slide rule) custom made for flying calculations to assist the pilots and the aircraft engineer. The standardized checklist was printed so that the crew could remember the many steps to preparing the plane for takeoff and flight. Intense training specific to this type of aircraft would be needed for the men now in basic training in the Army Air Force to operate the plane. Death was getting complicated.

The B-17 would continue to be modified throughout the Second World War. The new F model included improved Wright Cyclone engines, which provided greater maximum horsepower at the operational combat altitude of 25,000 feet. Among detail changes were improvements in armaments, with ammunition trace feed in place of containers, and additional armor protection for engines and crew members. An empty F model could weigh 34,000 pounds, and the given weight limit was now 56,500 pounds.[55] Her outside appearance remained almost unchanged from the E model except for the F's solid and clear Plexiglas nose.

READY FOR WAR

Her full name was B-17F-25-BO 41-24552. Because of the large demand for heavy bombers, some B-17s were being made by other companies, such as Vega and Douglas, at this point in the war. The Model F planes were constantly being modified, and she was part of a group of planes numbered 41-24540 to 41-24584. These Block Numbers were critically important to the crews who maintained the planes. It allowed the plane's crew chief to keep up the detailed evolutions of the B-17 and to know exactly which replacement parts might be required. Each aircraft had its own Maintenance Log Book, known as Form 41, which kept up with this "mod state" and the airplane's repair record.[56]

Number 552 was delivered to the Army Air Force August 4, 1942. From Seattle, she flew across the Rocky Mountains to Lowry Field in Denver, Colorado, landing there on August 7. On October 6 she flew to Hamilton Airfield on the Pacific Coast near Novato, California. She was ferried through Hawaii and finally arrived at her new home in Australia on November 5, 1942. Placed in the hands of the men of the 43rd Bomb Group, her role was straightforward: kill the enemy and bring her men back alive. Originally assigned to the 403rd Squadron, she was transferred to the 65th Squadron and flown to Milne Bay, New Guinea, November 23, 1942. For a time she returned to Australia on January 21, 1943, when she operated out of Mareeba Airfield. By May 11, 1943, she was back flying out of New Guinea at Port Moresby. She was designed, modified, and equipped to kill people—in this case, the military forces of the Empire of Japan, currently at war with her makers, the United States of America.[57]

Despite the massive modifications made to the B-17s coming off of the assembly lines, no one had envisioned the wide variety of climates and conditions in which the air force would be operating. The Southwest Pacific Theater had its own peculiar issues, and the maintenance crews were constantly struggling to keep the planes airworthy. The 43rd Bomb Group engineering section made forty-two engine changes, due to excessive oil consumption, on its B-17 Es and Fs during the first three months of operations from New Guinea. The Wright engines struggled to handle the high humidity and stress loads.[58]

A NEW NAME

Once B-17F-25-BO 41-24552 made it to Australia, her men gave her a new name. It would never replace her birth name, but this name reflected an attitude, a symbol of defiance. Combining the desperate conditions, the overwhelming odds, and the American sense of humor, an airplane's war name was intended to send a message. In this case #552 was prepared to take on the entire Japanese Empire single-handedly, including its head, Prime Minister Hideki Tojo. After one of the members of the unit used their artistic talents to paint a picture of a cartoon character holding a blunderbuss, #552 was formally christened by the men of the 43rd Bombardment Group the *Listen Here, Tojo!*

B-17F-25-BO 41-24552, "#552"

Chapter Six:

THE SOUTHWEST PACIFIC THEATER

PAUKENSCHLAG: GERMAN, NOUN, "TIMPANI ROLL," "DRUMBEAT"

Germany declared war on the United States on December 11, 1941, just four days after Pearl Harbor, and one week after that, Axis long-range Type IX submarines sailed for the coast of North America. Arriving on station in January 1942, they sank American merchant ships at an alarming rate, often in sight of civilians watching ashore. Guarding the American coastline were a collection of converted yachts, Coast Guard cutters, a few 1919 patrol boats, and some wooden submarine chasers. Called "Operation Paukenschlag" or "Operation Drumbeat" by the Germans, this long-range submarine sank ships and sowed panic along the eastern seaboard.

On February 18, 1942, the men of the 43rd Bombardment Group sailed from Boston Harbor. They had ridden by train from Maine, and the ship departed the harbor at noon for parts unknown.[59] As they headed out to the U-boat infested coastal waters, many on board believed they were headed to Europe to fight the Germans who were patrolling off their own coast. But as the *Queen Mary* turned south, the men had no idea where they were going. With almost 9,000 men and ship's crew aboard the *Queen Mary*, even the luxurious liner was robbed of its comfort.

George Carter of Headquarters Squadron recorded in his diary that he was quartered with eight other men in a stateroom, much better than the three thousand plus in the hold. On February 19, 1942, he wrote: "It is getting a good deal warmer so I know we must be headed south. We had our first life boat drill today."[60]

This was the first wartime mission of the *Queen Mary* as a troop transport. She was pressed into service because American men and material were needed to stem the tide of defeat around the world. On this day, the Japanese finished the conquest of Hong Kong on their victorious march across the Pacific. Even though the leadership of the nation had decided on a Germany-first strategy, events in the Pacific dictated that someone must be thrown at the Japanese to blunt their thrust. On board the *Queen Mary* were the main elements of the 64th and 65th Squadrons of the 43rd. Air crews, stripped to the minimum necessary to fly the planes, would ferry their planes to their destination, but the rest of the men went by boat. Despite the U-boat threat, the *Queen Mary* sailed alone, relying on her speed to protect her from the submarine menace. Slipping past the U-boats and racing past the Virginia coast and the Carolinas, the ship rounded Key West and then made the turn southwest for the long journey to Rio de Janeiro, Brazil, in South America. Despite the long time at sea for the men, many on their first transoceanic journey, she docked in Rio for two days only. For security reasons, all passengers stayed on-board the ship and were allowed no contact with anyone while they were in port. Setting sail once again, the *Queen Mary* passed Cape Town before finally arriving in Freemantle, Australia, concluding the interminable journey. The only item of note recorded by the unit historian was a shipboard fire on March 22, which was soon extinguished.[61] The last port of call for the men of the 43rd was Sydney, where they disembarked in a driving rain on March 28 after more than five weeks afloat. The journey covered 19,000 miles. The Germans claimed five times that their U-Boats had sunk the Queen Mary on her voyage.

Elements of the 43rd would continue to straggle into Australia for some time. General Kenney of Fifth Air Force fame would recall the scattered state of the unit when he found the 43rd Bomb Group in Australia: "All they had left was a flag and a couple of guys to hold it up."[62] Delmar may have traveled on the *Queen Mary*, but more likely, he flew with one of the B-17s being ferried to Australia. His records place him at Bangor Field, Maine, August 18, 1942, and he had a dentist appointment in Townsville, Australia, on October 16, 1942. At least once during his overseas service, he passed through Hawaii, which could have been a stopover on the flight from the USA to Australia. He probably took his pictures of the damage at Pearl Harbor while he was in transit to his assignment in Australia. B-17s had to island hop from remote airfield to remote airfield to transit the Pacific early in the war.[63] As planes arrived, the 43rd Bomb Group maintenance crews fixed any mechanical issues and began to assist the 19th Bombardment Group by repairing the battle damage on its B-17s. The 19th had started the war in the Philippines and gradually retreated all the way to Australia. Its men were exhausted, and their early model B-17s struggled in the wartime conditions.

When men of the 43rd Bomb Group arrived in Sydney, they were assigned to bivouac on the grounds of the Randwick Race Course. The Army Air Force supply situation continued to struggle with the demands of a world-wide war. No cots were available for the arriving men, so they slept on the floor. Since the unit had no airplanes at present, the soldiers kept occupied with exercise, a few lectures, and policing the area. The downside of staying at the race course soon became apparent when the men noticed large numbers of red welts on their bodies. The cause of the affliction was soon diagnosed as fleas. Even when cots arrived to get the men off of the floor, the fleas continued to plague them. At least the fleas were a distraction from the clouds of flies that swarmed them on a regular basis. Long food lines further added to the aggravation of the men as they adjusted to their new surroundings. After eating the food—much of it of the Australian variety and unfamiliar to the American palate—the men washed their mess kits in cold, dirty water. "By the middle of April . . . the men were pretty well used to the new customs. . . . Traffic keeping to the left, open trams, intermissions at the movies, and mutton were now commonplace things."[64]

Colonel Jim Pettus recalled that with the coming of Roger Ramey, at that time a colonel, to command the 43rd in Australia, things began to change. Ramey, a graduate of West Point, had started to pull together the scattered members of the unit. As the B-17s of the war-weary 19th Bomb Group came out of overhaul in Australia, the men of the 43rd began training on the reconditioned bombers. In Pettus' view, Ramey was further handicapped by the shortage of regular army officers and NCOs as he tried to prepare the unit for combat.[65]

It was here that the few experienced non-commissioned officers—the sergeants, like Delmar—proved their worth. With so many of the men new to the military, an "old hand" like Delmar was incalculable. Growing up at the Masonic Home of Virginia, Delmar had learned to look after those being bullied and take care of his younger brother and sister. As a staff sergeant, he now had to look after his men. The early success of the 43rd speaks well of the sergeants of the unit. For every newly appointed officer there is the first meeting with his sergeant. New lieutenants usually learn quickly what is "sergeant's business," and the good officers soon developed a trust in their senior NCOs like Delmar.

TOWNSVILLE, AUSTRALIA

When Americans travel to the tropics, three things confront them, and only three: heat, humidity, and insects. All other problems are corollaries to this. From Australia to New Guinea, the men were confronted with a menagerie of exotic insects and diseases, many of which they had never heard. Malaria was an ever-present problem, and the men were constantly told to take their Atabrine, "Be wise—Atabrinize."[66] The conditions in the Southwest Pacific area were so bad that even the Japanese soldiers complained about them. One Japanese soldier from the 26th Artillery Regiment would confide to his diary, "Our greatest enemy is the mosquito. Another is the Boeing."[67]

United States Air Force

As Townsville, Australia, became a hub of American activity in 1942, the 12th Army Station Hospital developed a steady stream of clients. The hospital opened for operation in March of 1942, and Staff Sergeant Delmar Dotson was an early customer and had a dental exam there October

16, 1942. A modern dentist who evaluated his dental records found that "Gold foil was used regularly back then and I think that is what we are seeing. Gold foil is exactly that—a soft malleable foil that is packed into cavity preparations where the decay was removed. I just can't figure out why they were not recorded in his dental record."[68]

The seedy reputation of Townsville notwithstanding, one reporter from a local newspaper painted an almost idyllic picture of life there during the war. The painting was entitled, "One Sunday Afternoon in Townsville 1942" by Roy Hodkinson and showed Allied soldiers on what could be a relaxing Sunday outing at the lake. This perception would be picked up by the Japanese and used for propaganda purposes, and they implied that while the Australian soldiers were away fighting the Nazis, the Americans were living the high life back home in Australia.

Escaping the fleas of the race track in Sydney may have seemed good at first, but the move to Townsville presented its own challenges. Townsville was rapidly becoming a major staging area for Allied troops

Roy Hodkison[69]

on the move toward New Guinea. Though Townsville was somewhat "behind the lines," the Japanese did manage to bomb the area with long-range flying boats on occasion.

WILLING. ABLE. READY. (43RD BOMB GROUP MOTTO)

The 65th Squadron, now beginning flight operations out of Townsville, was finally ready to strike back at the Japanese. The 43rd Bomb Group had only been in existence for a year and a half and arrived in Australia a matter of months before. However, the Japanese were steadily progressing closer to Australia. Not only would a Japanese landing on the continent of Australia be devastating for Allied morale but would also greatly complicate the efforts of the US forces in building up their strength to push back against the almost unimpeded Japanese march across the Pacific.

On November 22, 1942, the 65th Squadron went to war. Seven B-17s took off from Townsville to attack Japanese shipping near Lae, New Guinea. According to historian Bruce Hoy, this may have been the first combat mission of the B-17 41-24552 *Listen Here, Tojo!*, #552. If so, then this would be an incredible coincidence since the last mission of the *Listen Here, Tojo!* would be to bomb Lae just before the Australian infantry occupied it. The records of the Combined Headquarters in Townsville recorded that plane #552 (*Listen Here, Tojo!*) turned back before reaching the target due to mechanical problems. The six remaining bombers attacked the convoy, and one B-17 was shot down. Turning back without dropping any ordinance marked an inauspicious beginning for #552.[70]

The organization of the 65th Squadron was typical for a bombing squadron: twelve bombers plus the flight crews and the all-important ground crews. However, at this point in the war, when the squadron was assigned a bombing mission, it seldom meant that twelve bombers made the attack. In the Southwest Pacific, squadrons rarely had their full complement of planes available on any given day because of the combat damage and the difficulty of flying complex machinery in the tropics. The early missions from Townsville would sometimes entail the few available bombers flying to a landing field in Port Moresby, New Guinea, known as Seven Mile Drome. Airfields around Port Moresby were named by how far they were from the port. Three Mile Drome was three miles away, Seven Mile Drome was seven miles away, and Twelve Mile Drome was twelve miles away.[71] Seven Mile Drome was also called Jackson Field and had been named after a Royal Australian Air Force pilot (RAAF) who had been killed, Squadron Leader John Francis Jackson.

The 43rd's B-17s would take off from Townsville, Australia, and fly to Port Moresby, New Guinea, where they would land at dusk and spend the night, a dangerous proposition with Japanese air raids afoot. In the morning, the B-17s would take off from Jackson Field in New Guinea, bomb their targets, and return to Townsville, Australia, to refuel and rearm. This arrangement greatly complicated the efforts of the 43rd to strike at Japanese targets and further exacerbated the supply shortages plaguing every aspect of the units' operations.

The American units at the end of the supply chain in the Southwest Pacific learned to scavenge and improvise what they needed. Australian military equipment was merged with American materials to supply the needs of the units. General Kenney wrote, "We couldn't get anything out of the United States for some time, so we were modifying the Australian eleven-second delay fuses into four- to five-second delay."[72] These fuses were then placed in the American-made bomb casings. Kenney began asking for any military equipment not wanted by other theaters of war to be shipped to him. Not a very satisfying arrangement, but at least they were taking the fight to the enemy.

As the buildup of American forces progressed, VIPs began to appear. President Roosevelt sent Lt. Cmdr. Lyndon B. Johnson to the Southwest Pacific on a fact-finding tour and expected him to report back on the morale of the fighting men in the theater. It, no doubt, would have amazed Staff Sergeant Dotson to know that his kid sister would dance with Johnson at a Presidential Ball twenty years later. Carrie Lee, by then a fixture on the Washington social scene, would like President Johnson's politics but not his dancing.

Another celebrity finally made his way to Port Moresby in late 1942. World War I Ace of Aces for the Americans, Eddie Rickenbacker, was on a fact-finding mission for the Secretary of War. Rickenbacker had been delayed and presumed dead when the B-17 on which he was flying ran out of fuel and ditched in the Pacific Ocean. After three weeks on the open ocean in rubber boats, Rickenbacker and the others were rescued. Recuperating quickly, Rickenbacker decided to continue his mission to visit the American units, learn about their challenges, and, most importantly, see if the rumors of low morale were true. Despite the reason for his visit, the appearance of Captain Eddie Rickenbacker, America's World War I Ace of Aces, was a highlight for the men, especially the fighter pilots.[73] When Rickenbacker got home, he said of the soldiers in New Guinea, "If only our people back home could know what those boys are doing for us and our future generations, I think we would take this war much more seriously." The war in New Guinea was "kill or be killed, the quick and the dead."[74]

Ferocious biting insects, poisonous snakes, malaria, dengue fever, hot and humid weather, and monsoon rains lasting from November to March were what tail gunner Peter S. Owens remembered about Northern Australia.[75] Two months in New Guinea caused each soldier a typical weight loss of fifteen to thirty pounds. Most units could only stay there two months before illness compelled them to be rotated back to Australia. Whether Mareeba, Townsville, or Torrens Creek, the story was the same; the conditions caused more distress at this point than the Japanese. The mosquitos were reputed to be the size of airplanes and with a bite to match. One familiar story of the size of the insects involved an airplane refueling crew that was in action after dark. The crew saw something come down at the end of the runway as they began the refueling operation. They had loaded twenty gallons of gasoline into the thing before they realized that it wasn't a P-39 fighter; it was a mosquito.[76]

Meanwhile in New Guinea, things were moving from desperate to worse. The Japanese were crossing over the spine of the Owen Stanley Mountains, headed for Port Morseby. The path, known as the Kokoda Trail, is considered almost impassable even today. The conditions were so harsh that resupply was next to impossible. Some reports stated that Japanese soldiers, driven mad by the lack of food and the overwhelming jungle, resorted to cannibalism whenever they captured patrolling Australian soldiers.[77] With Allied resources stretched past the breaking point, intense pressure was placed on 5th Air Force General George C. Kenney to use the air power under his command to halt the disastrous setbacks in New Guinea and stop the Japanese advance on Port Moresby.

THE GENERAL

For George Kenney, this was his second world war. As a fighter pilot in the First World War, Lt. Kenney flew seventy-five missions and shot down two German planes. After years of studying aeronautical development and aerial warfare, Kenney was appointed commander of all Allied Air Forces in the Southwest Pacific in August 1942.[78] When Kenney took over what became known as the Fifth Air Force, he was shocked not only at the state of affairs in the theater but also with the casual way Washington talked about Australia being overrun by the Japanese. Kenney's orders were to maintain a sort of "strategic defensive." Once again, all of the prewar preparation and planning lost out to the exigencies of the moment.[79]

Delmar and his men had struggled to maintain their daily existence, let alone fight a war. They were eating the Australian rations known as "M and Vs" for meat and vegetables. The leftover tin cans came in handy as well. Since they had few reserves of sheet aluminum, the crews used the flattened tin cans to repair bullet holes on their bombers.[80] When bread arrived at Port Moresby, it had weevils and flies cooked into it. What food they had, Australian or American, was often dehydrated and tasted bad. They could always fish for something fresh. Of course they had to be careful of their bored fellow soldiers, who entertained themselves by shark hunting with hand grenades.[81]

The exhausted men of the 19th Bomb Group rotated home to the United States; they had been fighting since the war's onset. Most Southwest Pacific men were so broken down health-wise that even after a return stateside to recuperate, they never deployed overseas again. As General Kenney saw his precious crews rotate home, he contacted Washington incessantly for replacements, which were slow in coming. As disease and combat took their toll, the fighting strength of the 5th Air Force was at a low ebb. Kenney realized that as far as heavy bomber units, the 43rd was it. "That's all I had, there wasn't any more."[82]

On December 13, 1942, #552 *Listen Here, Tojo!* was in action bombing Japanese destroyers in the Solomon Sea. On the mission, the #552 and the other B-17s not only had to fend off enemy fighters but a new weapon as well. The five Japanese fighters flew over the American planes and dropped aerial bombs on them. These weapons were designed to explode amid the formation of the bombers, and the shrapnel could then cause massive damage. The challenge of getting the aerial bombs to explode at just the right time proved too great, and no aerial-bomb damage was reported by the American crews. The weekly status report for the 65th Squadron stated that six DDs (destroyers) were bombed and four of the bombs were observed to fall within seventy-five feet of the ships, but no damage was observed. After the bombs were dropped, B-17 *Listen Here, Tojo!* and the formation returned to the airbase in

Mareeba, North Queensland, Australia, but one bomber was forced to ditch. When the bomber ditched, crew member Lt. Howard Eberly, the copilot on this particular mission, survived the ditching of the airplane. Eberly and one other crew member swam fourteen hours before they were finally able to reach dry land. Eventually, they returned to the unit and resumed flying missions.[83]

It was proving difficult for the B-17s to bomb Japanese shipping effectively. One reason for this difficulty was the lack of bomb sights. Bomb sights, like so many other basic items, were in short supply, and some bombers were not equipped with them. On these missions, the lead B-17 would have a bomb sight, and upon its release, all the other planes would release their bombs. If the lead plane was off, everyone would be off. To add to the difficulty, the B-17 was designed to bomb stationary targets, and it had not been envisioned that the planes would be used against fast-moving ships, with the ability to turn and dodge away from the bomb patterns. New tactics would be called for in order for the B-17s to continue antiship bombing.

New Guinea was a unique theater in World War II in many ways. Even though it was a single island, the steep Owen Stanley Mountains ran through the central portion of the island like a raised spine. Other than aboriginal tribes who inhabited the interior, all others stayed close to the coastline. The airfields in the jungle became like islands in the ocean; they were clearings of civilization surrounded by inhospitable vastness. Parachuting over "friendly" territory was no guarantee that an airman would survive long enough to return to friendly forces. Natives, rumored to still eat human flesh (which they called long pork) roamed the inhospitable jungle. Any cut or scrape could be life threatening because of the hot tropical climate. At that stage of the war, the crews had little or no jungle survival training to know how to live off of the land.

With the coming of the new year of 1943, on January 8 and 9 the 43rd was in action bombing a Japanese resupply convoy. Number 552, *Listen Here, Tojo!* flew as a part of these raids. The missions on the 8th and then on the 9th both saw a bomb strike on a transport. Delmar and the 65th Squadron continued their nomadic existence by flying out of yet another airfield. The Iron Range Airfield in Australia had been the location of a gold mining operation. Since the dirt had a high gold content, the landing strip was called the Golden Runway.[84]

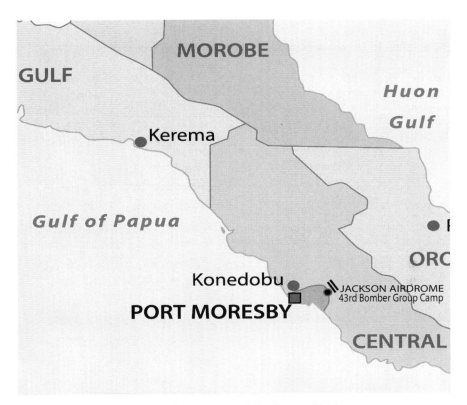

Port Moresby area and Jackson Airdrome,
new home of the 43rd Bomb Group

MOVE TO NEW GUINEA

The operation tempo slowed down for Delmar and the 43rd Bomb Group in January because the group was moving, yet again, but this time to New Guinea. No longer just a staging area, Port Moresby, New Guinea, and its Jackson Field would be the new home of the 43rd Bomb Group and the 65th Squadron.

In the 1880s, Germany had annexed the area of eastern New Guinea in its bid to become a colonial power like England. Australia also tried to claim eastern New Guinea as its own, and the result was that Germany controlled the northeastern half of the island and Australia influenced the southeastern half. At the conclusion of World War I, when Germany surrendered and gave up its overseas territories, Australia took over administrative control of the entire eastern half of the island. The

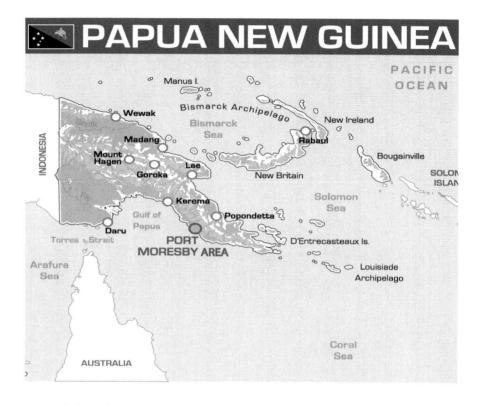

Port Moresby area and Jackson Airdrome, new home of the 43rd Bomb Group

city of Port Moresby rested on the southeastern half of the island, close to Australia, and eventually became the capital of what is today known as Papua, New Guinea.

Port Moresby was considered a place of beauty, until you got close to it. The sunsets were beautiful, and the green canopy looked serene. When preparing to land in New Guinea, air crews noticed a strange smell as they neared the landing strip. It was as if the fetid stench of rotting vegetation climbed up to meet them and pull them into its arms. The smell was like the humidity; it embraced you, permeated every pore of your skin, and clung to your soul. The humid dampness never left you. In New Guinea, you stayed wet until the rainy season when you got wetter. The flies were so bad that the constant waving of the hand in front of the face was known as the "New Guinea salute." As soon as your food was served, a blanket of flies covered it. You only hoped that you could swat them away long enough to avoid eating the flies with the meal. The weather was oppressive as well. The heavy cloud cover prompted a saying among the pilots: "In New Guinea the clouds have rocks in them."[85] Low clouds around the spinal mountain range of the island, the Owen Stanley Mountains, meant that passing through the mountain passes on a cloudy day was always a tricky proposition.

The atmospheric conditions made St. Elmo's fire appear on the B-17s at times. New crews were alarmed to see a bright blue or violet glow appear on their wings, or in some cases, on the spinning tips of the propellers. Caused by an electrical field ionizing the air molecules around the metal parts of the airplane during events like thunderstorms, this apparition further unnerved the air crews as they tried to cope with all that was New Guinea.

The Owen Stanley Mountains 2012, author's collection

The military did its best with limited information to prepare the men for the horrors of New Guinea. A booklet passed out to the troops, *A Pocket Guide to New Guinea and the Solomons*, gave a wide range of useful advice, such as, "On this job, you'll know the South Seas a lot better than when you looked at Dotty Lamour's sarong in the movies back home." And "You don't need to be told that campaigning in these islands is no picnic—you're often steamy and sweaty and muddy; in fact conditions are about as bad as on any battlefront in the world. But the islands are not all bad by any means."[86] On weather, the guide informed the interested reader that the thermometer could reach as high as 125 to 135 degrees, but it was usually cooler along the coast. Rainfall averaged 40 inches a year in Port Moresby and up to 165 inches a year elsewhere. Besides the insects, soldiers were told to beware of the leeches whenever they came in contact with water. When the leeches attached themselves, the troops could use a lighted cigarette, a lighter, a spit of tobacco juice, soapy water, gasoline, or a pinch of salt to make them let go. A warning was made to not pull the leeches off, or the resulting sore could cause a serious infection. For food, they could watch the birds, and whatever they ate, the soldiers could probably eat. To talk to the locals, they needed to learn Pidgin English. Useful phrases were included, such as, "House peck-peck, ee stop where?" which meant, "Where is the toilet?" Useful to know when fighting in the jungle.[87]

THE ENEMY

By the end of January, mission tempo picked up where it had left off. On one of the missions, ball turret gunner Arthur Jingozian was on board the B-127 41-2638 *I'm Willing*, flying a reconnaissance mission over Rabaul. Jingozian and the crew barely made it back from the heavily defended harbor after fighting off the Japs. Jingozian would become no stranger to in-flight drama as a correspondent for a West Australian newspaper (Perth, Australia) wrote:

> Nightmare Flight: Desperate Task to Release Bomb (from Our Special Representative)
>
> SOMEWHERE IN NEW GUINEA. June 21.—First-Lt W. Baldwin, of Pennsylvania, was worried by more than the Japanese and the tropical weather during Saturday's pre-dawn raid on Vunakanau aerodrome at Rabaul. He almost lost one of his crew through the yawning chasm of the open bomb-bay. His bombardier had to wrestle with a loose bomb which was discovered only by accident lying on the bomb-bay floor and to conclude a nightmare flight one of his engines was visited by "gremlins" and threatened to set the bomber aflame.

During Baldwin's run over the target area his Fortress was attacked 5 times by enemy night fighters. The worst experience of all that crowded into a couple of dreadful hours was the loose bomb. No sooner had this playmate of the devil been cleared when a second bomb was discovered in its rack. Stubbornly fixed, it failed to release even with the use of all emergency devices so the ball turret gunner, Sgt. Arthur Jingozian, of East Bridgewater (Mass.) straddled the gaping space between the bomb-bay catwalk and the fuselage to release the bomb by hand.

Only about 5ft tall, young Jingozian found it all he could do to reach across the chasm which threatened a horrible death about 8,000 ft. below. Suddenly when the rest of the crew were watching Jingozian's desperate task the Fortress gave a sickening lurch and Jingozian lost his footing.

There was a freezing moment of despair until young Jingozian seized the foot of a fuselage column and anxious hands reached out to haul him back to safety just as the bomb dropped clear. This however was not the end of the crew's troubles. During the last hour before reaching base one engine began to run rough and threatened to explode when the engineer found he could not feather the propeller. Everyone was ready to bail out on the order, but their luck held and they returned sorely shaken from an unforgettable flight.[88]

The Port of Rabaul, captured by the Japanese from the Australians, had been turned into the main Japanese base in the South Pacific. Only 498 miles (806 kilometers) from Port Moresby, the base would increasingly become the target of numerous raids by the 43rd. By late 1943, the harbor was a veritable shooting gallery for the Japanese antiaircraft gunners. Eight 12.7 cm antiaircraft guns ringed the harbor, along with fifteen 12 cm guns and over 250 guns of smaller caliber. The ships anchored in the harbor added their guns to the mass of firepower directed at any bombers foolish enough to make Rabaul their target.[89]

Ultimately, there were three airfields around the harbor with their own antiair defense measures. These airfields, Vunakanau, Lakunai, and later Rapopo, would also become frequent targets for the bombers of the 43rd.[90]

As if the antiaircraft defenses were not enough, Japanese fighters also posed a constant threat. For the Japanese fighter pilots, shooting down a B-17 was a difficult proposition under normal circumstances. The B-17s were nicknamed "Fortresses" for a reason, and they sported ten or more .50 caliber machine guns in rotating turrets and other positions from tail to nose. The design and construction of the stout plane meant that the enemy fighter pilot needed a large number of hits from his machine guns to cause critical damage. If the Jap fighters stayed too close too long, they paid a dear price at the hands of the B-17s' gunners. Crack shots like machine-gunner Sgt. Joe Ferraiolo took full advantage of all opportunities to use their skills and deadly machine-gun fire to bring down the Japanese fighters. On March 11, 1943, *The Argus* newspaper of Melbourne, Australia, ran an article about the resilience of the B-17 when under attack. Ferraiolo and the other gunners of the crew waged a desperate gun battle with the enemy over the vast expanse of the ocean.

> Fortress Home with 4 Wounded: Attacked by 9 Zeros
> From Geoffrey Hutton, "Argus" War Correspondent
>
> SOMEWHERE IN NEW GUINEA. Wed: With 4 members of her crew wounded and a long string of bullet holes extending from the nose to the tail, a Flying Fortress made a perfect landing at an advanced Allied base yesterday after a lone battle against 9 Zeros. Four of the Zeros were destroyed and a fifth disappeared into a cloud with a hundred bullets in it before the attackers broke off the action.
>
> The 4 wounded men were the pilot, co-pilot, navigator, and the bombardier, the only officers in the crew. After the pilot had been hit in the back and thigh the co-pilot took over, flew the plane home, and landed it, although he had a Japanese bullet

within an inch of his jugular vein. Sgt. William Madison, of Oregon, the engineer, took the co-pilot's seat. All 4 wounded men are in hospital and doing well.

"We were jumped by the Zeros as we left a cloud over Gasmata, where we were doing an armed reconnaissance," said Sgt Leonard Williams, of Brooklyn, the photographer. "They were in range before we had warning, and they came on in pairs attacking from either side. The cloud was too thin to give protection, so we let go our bombs and took on all 9 Zeros. One burst of a Zero's machinegun cut a pattern of holes along the fuselage, but the shots missed all vital parts, and only knocked out the inter-communication telephone, which is used for fire control. Sgt. Mike Andrade got 2 Zeros and Sgt. Joe Ferraiolo and Pte Dave Eckholt got one each for certain. The fight lasted 15 to 20 minutes before they sheared off."

"The pilot was weak from loss of blood, and we were all giving first aid to the wounded, but he tried to get back to the controls to bring the plane in. He couldn't make it, but the co-pilot had things well under control flying for 2 hours, and then bringing the ship down in spite of the bullet in his neck. Although she has so many holes in her the plane is sound enough and will be flying again soon."[91]

Lt. Carroll Guy, who flew with the 65th Squadron later in the war, recalled that whenever they landed with wounded and dead crewmen aboard, the ground personnel would get the flight crews away from the airplane as soon as possible. They didn't want the crews to see the bodies pulled from the aircraft. If a plane crashed on landing, the other planes would be kept in a holding pattern until the crew was removed from the wrecked plane.[92] In spite of the horrors of war, the men of the 43rd kept flying. Amazing accounts of heroism would be replicated time and time again by the crew members of the 43rd Bomb Group and their B-17 bombers.

Zeros at Twelve o'clock USAF

Chapter Seven:

ABOVE AND BEYOND

As the rainy season ebbed, the pace of operations picked up for the 43rd Bomb Group and Delmar. The year 1943 saw the Fifth Air Force under General Kenney begin to turn the tide on the Japanese military. The army and navy forces had seen their momentum blunted by the delaying action of Allied forces and then were surprised at the naval Battle of Coral Sea and the land battle for the previously unknown island of Guadalcanal. The bombers

Logo of the 65th Squadron, 43rd Bomb Group during the B-17 era

of the Fifth Air Force sprung a nasty surprise on Japanese naval craft with the advent of skip bombing. Flying a few hundred feet above sea level, bombers, including the bulky B-17s, would drop their bombs, "skipping" them on the water into the sides of the Japanese ships. General Kenney brought the strategy and tactics of the Fifth Air Force to a new level of competence, even sophistication. The Japanese ground forces were retreating before the Australian and American infantry, who were backed up by the innovative Fifth Air Force. One example of American ingenuity involved cutting a truck in half, transporting the halves, and then welding the truck back together once the planes delivered their cargo to the target area.[93]

On February 1, 1943, Lt. Hal Winfrey was at the controls of the *Listen Here, Tojo!* on a photo-reconnaissance mission along the northeastern coast of New Guinea, from the towns of Buna to Salamaua. Pilot Winfrey wrote in his diary that it was the quietest mission he had yet flown.[94] On the Weekly Status Report for the 43rd Bomb Group, it was noted: "Port Moresby to Vitiaz Straits to Open Bay to Wide Bay to St. George to Buka Passage to 7 degrees South Latitude 155 degrees 20' East to Wide Bay to Hood Point to Port Moresby."[95] The next day one of the B-17 machine gunners, Jennings Messer, fought off enemy fighters on a mission to Rabaul and was later awarded the Silver Star for the mission.[96][97] On February 9, Staff Sergeant Ferraialo was again in action aboard the *Listen Here, Tojo!* on a nine-hour reconnaissance mission. The Weekly Status Report for this period of time noted that some of the hundred-pound general purpose bombs had been fitted with whistles. The assumption was that the screaming sound of the falling bombs would spread terror among the Japanese ground forces. On April 2, Jennings Messer received another commendation for bravery. This time he was awarded the Air Medal for a bombing mission to Kavieng. The Weekly Status Report noted that one B-17 dropped its bombs by hand due to a mechanical malfunction.[98]

Even with success in the field, the men of the 43rd were exhausted. The jungle conditions—the men slept in tents on dirt floors—and exotic diseases, on top of the stress of war, gave way to bone-numbing exhaustion. Casualty rates were through the roof. It was hard enough to patch the planes back together, but crews had to be patched together as well. Even simple things like the wrong food for flight crews brought on more suffering. The Australian rations of beans were found to have a debilitating effect when the men reached higher altitudes. Gastronomic distress aside, at least the air crews got to leave the heat and humidity on days that they flew. The ground crews were trapped in the malarial cesspool of jungle odors and voracious insects. Simple jobs like turning over the propellers before engine start were a problem. Before the B-17 engines were started, the ground crews would turn the propeller blades by hand—turning "9 blades"—and then the engine would be started. The sharp edges of the propellers, when heated to tropical temperatures, made everything painful.

WE CAN'T LOSE

Delmar, temporarily assigned to headquarters, wrote to little sister Carrie Lee to give the best update he could without the censors stepping in.

Miss Carrie Lee Nelson
Memorial Hall Nurse's Home
Richmond, Va.

T/Sgt. Delmar Dotson
HQ 43rd Bomb Group
A.P.O. 929 San Francisco, Calif.

Feb. 15, 1943
Somewhere in New Guinea

Dear "Sis,"

I'm still waiting for that blond you promised me. "Sis," if you don't write and let me know just what you have received from me I'm going to punch you in the nose. I'm sending some pictures in a couple of days.

I wrote to Glenn [older brother Glenn Dotson] yesterday. He was in the Mid-West somewhere. I sure would like to see him, it has been a long time since I have seen him.

I have some nice pictures of the natives here and believe me . . . they are well built.

Tell all my friends hello. Tell "Shady" I dreamed he and I got captured by the Japs.

Your Brother,
Delmar

Delmar's mention of Shady probably referred to a mutual friend of theirs from the days at the Masonic Home of Virginia. As would be true of most (if not all) of Delmar's squadron mates in New Guinea were the ever-present thoughts of home and girls. In his letter to little sister Carrie Lee, Delmar demanded that she pay up the blond she owed him. As if on cue, one of Delmar's next letters went to an old flame, Clara, who just happened to be in nursing school with Carrie Lee.

April 9, 1943
Clara Whisnant

Look Here, You Beautiful Thing,

Remember you, I should say I do. I was even thinking, while I was talking to you, 'Boy, would I like to take you out. But of course we Dotsons are very bashful.

Yes, I would like to be back in the hills just like you say. But I would like to be where you were. Then I could tell you of my travels. No, you have not heard them all. "Sis" only hears a few.

By the way, if one of these days if I return could I or could we continue where we left off? Heck I tried (B) you know about Mom. It did not work. Tell my "Sis" to go to ?????

As Ever,
Delmar

Clara Whisnant (left)
and Carrie Lee Dotson,
Richmond, VA, 1943

SILVER STAR MISSION

Delmar Dotson was flying into trouble and he knew it. Not since his great-grandfather Tandy Branham chased down his stolen horse single-handedly had a member of Delmar's family taken on such odds. Events had not turned out well for Tandy when he rode into the ambush by Alf Killen and the Yankee Home Guards. Events were not going well for Sgt. Dotson as he rode into the ambush by the Japs at Rabaul.

Back home, Monday was the start of the work week, but war had few weekends for frontline troops. A few days before, the Detroit Red Wings had swept the Boston Bruins four games to zero to win the Stanley Cup. An arena of ice would have seemed a fantasy to the men of the 43rd by this time in the war. Delmar wrote home to his older sister Laura (now Spradlin), living in New Lexington, Ohio.

Mrs. Laura Spradlin
New Lexington, Ohio
Passed by US Army Examiner 16353

T/Sgt. Delmar Dotson
65th SQ. 43rd Bomb GP
A.P.O. 929 San Francisco, Calif.
April 9, 1943

SOMEWHERE IN NEW GUINEA

Hello "Sister,"

You know your big brother is working hard as heck to win this war. So don't get excited, we cannot lose with me at the wheel.

How is my "Sister" these days? Fine I hope. And how is the world for your husband, fine also?

I'll bet your children are big enough to be going dancing by now. Right, well tell them Delmar said, "Everything's O.K. here and for them to keep everything O.K. there."

Love,
Delmar

THE BRIEFING

The mission for Monday, April 12, 1943, called for a multiplane raid on Rabaul. The raid had to be timed so that the planes arrived over the target at dawn. This meant a nighttime take off. Flying B-17F #41-24548 would be pilot 1st Lt. Ted Crawford Jr. Assigned to the Crawford crew for this mission would be 1st Lt. John L. Gibbs-copilot, 2nd Lt. Max H. Mayer-bombardier, 2nd Lt. John G. Thompson-navigator, Tech. Sgt Delmar Dotson-Flight Engineer, Staff Sgt. Robert F. Watson-lower turret gunner, Sgt. Joseph Shaparus-waist gunner, and Cpl. Richard L. Kelley.

Crawford and Mayer had flown together before. In his account of the war published in 1944, Crawford reported that, "My new bombardier, 2nd Lt. Max Mayer, was a short paunchy Tennessean—we called him 'Memphis Max.'"[99] Of all the crew members, Delmar seemed to be the one added for this mission. Crawford's regular flight engineer, Ritenour, had been assigned to ground duty after the March 1943 Battle of the Bismark Sea.

RAID ON RABAUL

Crews briefed, planes fueled, and bombed-up preparations for the mission were complete. Nine B-17s were scheduled for the strike mission. Just ahead of Crawford's plane, Major Kenneth McCullar prepared to move. McCullar, now a squadron commander, was a living legend in the 43rd. Holder of numerous decorations, the popular commander had taken the best the Japs could send at him and had given back with interest. As soon as McCullar's plane began to move, Crawford revved his engines in preparation for takeoff. The full load of eight 500-pound bombs weighed the plane down, but the anxious engines throbbed, ready to move.

As McCullar's plane rolled down the runway and into the air, Crawford pushed his throttles wide open and started down the strip. The next moment McCullar's plane burst into flames, tilted to one side, and dove into the earth. The impact detonated the bombs and the full-load aviation fuel sent fiery bolts into the air. Later it was believed that a wallaby had run onto the airfield in front of McCullar's plane, was hit by the number two engine, and led to the explosion. Flight Engineer Delmar was stationed right behind the pilots, saw the explosion, and realized they were headed right into the inferno. Crawford pulled the nose of his plane up as much as he dared and flew right over the burning bomber. Crawford, Dotson, and the crew had little time to dwell on this blow to unit morale, as they had a mission to fly.

Finally reaching altitude, Crawford's bomber set up for the Valley of Death, known as Rabaul. About an hour after leaving Port Moresby, the oil pressure dropped on the number three engine. Later they would find out that an oil line had broken. Even with the improved supply situation, ground crews were still scavenging parts from wrecked planes. Flight Engineer Dotson worked with the pilots to feather the propeller on number three. This meant that the propeller blades would be rotated so that they did not spin out of control and destroy the engine. At this stage of the war, several B-17s had been unable to feather a prop on a damaged engine, and the results had been catastrophic. The crew now had the perfect excuse to call off their mission and return to base. Attacking Rabaul was dicey enough under normal conditions, but with one engine already out, they should turn back to base. It was eight hundred miles to Rabaul, and now their airspeed would be seriously compromised. Besides, the loss of McCullar and his crew must have been a gut punch to the men.

NO TURNING BACK

According to Crawford, "I asked the rest of the fellows if they thought we ought to return to base. They were all for going on."[100] No sooner had they made this decision than the weather decided to turn nasty. The formation hit a heavy tropical thunderstorm and the planes scattered. Now alone and with mechanical trouble, they continued the mission.

High-formation flying was largely discarded in the Pacific by this time. This picture of European B-17s flying by the hundreds and bombing from 20,000 feet didn't apply to the Southwest Pacific Theater. As daylight dawned on Rabaul, the first B-17s should have hit the target already. Sometime about 7:00 a.m. local time the Crawford crew found themselves over Rabaul at 6,000 feet . . . alone. They made their Rabaul target the Lakanai airdrome and flew on with a clear sight of the objective. Bombardier Mayer released the bombs and soon terrific explosions were observed. Direct hits racked ammunitions dumps and oil dumps. Debris was thrown hundreds of feet into the air. Almost three hundred guns opened up on the lone three-engine fortress. Holes appeared in the wings and fuselage but nothing vital was hit. All eyes were alert for enemy fighters but none appeared. They made it. If only they could make it home.

Crawford now had to coax as much power out of the remaining engines as possible. The plane was lighter with the release of the bombs, so that helped. Ahead were the Owen Stanley Mountains that were never sympathetic to planes that couldn't make altitude. Gradually climbing to 16,000 feet, the plane now entered the area where ice could form on the wings. On this particular plane, the rubber deicer boots on the front were not working. The tropical heat had rotted the rubber, and no replacements were to be had. Clouds now closed in, and the pilots were relying on their instruments. Clouds in New Guinea had rocks in them, so they said, meaning the clouds obscured the high mountaintops. Visibility dropped to a few hundred feet. Flying in a damaged plane in a gray soup must have made the crew claustrophobic. The ice began to pile up on the wings, weighing the plane down. Crawford knew he didn't dare drop down below the ice zone because he would likely impact one of the mountaintops, and that would end the mission in a hurry.

Making it through the mountain passes, Crawford dropped down to a lower altitude to let the ice melt off the wings, but this day Mother Nature was clearly on the side of the Japanese. The plane ran right into another tropical rain storm, but this one had something extra . . . tropical hail. Even for these veterans of the tropics, this was something new. The hail was egg sized and hammered the plane with resounding fury. Soon the machine guns began to be dismounted by the force of the hail strikes. The vibrations sent ammo cans rattling around the inside of the fuselage. Delmar, checking on the plane and crew, watched helplessly as the Plexiglas of his top turret cracked with spider-like beauty.

Despite the best the Japanese and the weather could throw at them, Crawford landed the plane back at Jackson Field. Once back in his tent, Crawford's squadron commander, Major Harry Hawthorne, entered and said concisely, "Good going, Crawford."[101] As for Delmar, well, he was mentioned in the newspaper. Great-Grandfather Tandy Branham would have been proud.

Kingsport Times, Monday August 30, 1943
Pound Soldier Wins Silver Star Fighting Japs

Allied Headquarters in the Southwest Pacific—AP—The crew of a Flying Fortress that made a daylight raid on Rabaul, New Britain, last April 12, with only three engines working and no other American planes in sight, has been awarded Silver Stars for gallantry in action.

First Lt. William Crawford, Jr., pilot, of Niles, Ohio was awarded an Oak Leaf Cluster in lieu of a second Silver Star.

Silver Stars went to First Lt. John L. Gibbs, Ovett, Miss., Second Lts. Max H. Mayer, Memphis, Tenn., and Jack G. Thompson of Fort Pierce, Fla.; Tech Sgt. Delmar Dotson, Pound, Va., Staff Sgt. Robert F. Watson (Route 1) Roanoke, W. Va.; Sgt. Joseph Shapura, Westville, Ill.; and Corp. Richard L. Kelley, Saginaw, Mich.[102]

Chapter Eight:

PERSEVERE

The word used for her was tired. Tired is a word generally thought of to describe a human ailment, but in this case it fit the airplane as well. The *Listen Here, Tojo!*, #552, had amassed a lot of hours in the air, not just any hours but combat hours. On April 4 she had just crossed over the Owen Stanley Mountains when two of her four engines developed trouble and started running rough. One of the props had to be feathered ,and with the other engine running at reduced power, she had to return to Jackson Airfield.[103]

The crew of *Listen Here, Tojo!* had been sent to conduct a reconnaissance starting at Wide Bay on the south coast of New Britain (the island that held the Japanese installation of Rabaul). She made it back over the mountains only because she already had enough altitude to trade height for distance. With another crew manning her, she had also flown on the April 12 mission to Rabaul (the one for which Delmar had been nominated for a Silver Star). She had targeted the airfield at Rapapo at Rabaul, but mechanical issues meant that the bombs in the bomb bay wouldn't release. Captain William Smith was flying #552 that day, and he took her away from the Rabaul Airfield to fly over St. George's Channel. A submarine was spotted in the water below, and the bombs, mechanical issue now fixed, were salvoed. The crew reported that the Japanese submarine received superficial damage from the blasts.[104]

AIR RAID AT JACKSON FIELD

As an NCO, Delmar continued to take care of his men, and he did his part to lift the spirits of the unit. Ongoing construction made life more tolerable for the men of the 65th Squadron and the 43rd as a whole. More buildings now had screening and concrete floors. However, none of that mattered when the air raid alert sounded and the men had to scramble to the slit trenches until the Japanese bombs had done their work. As if losing sleep wasn't bad enough, in the trenches, the men were now fodder for the massive army of insects looking for a meal. One pilot commented that you could hear the Jap planes from far off because their engines were not synchronized. Though the raids usually didn't cause great destruction, the rain of deadly bombs could be unnerving.

One night as the enemy planes were moving overhead in their bombing runs across the airdrome and the antiaircraft guns were booming away, the men of the 43rd hunkered down in the trenches began to hear an unusual noise in the few lulls in the din of battle. As they listened closely, some of the men figured out that someone had taken a trumpet into their trench and was now playing away. In fact, as the raid died out and the ring of bombs faded away, the tune became recognizable; they realized that someone had been playing the Ink Spot's big hit, "I Don't Want to Set the World on Fire." The men in the slit trenches knew immediately who was playing that trumpet. No one could, or even would, play that tune in the midst of exploding bombs but Technical Sergeant Delmar Dotson. Dotson was at it again.[105]

TSgt. Delmar Dotson April 28, 1943. This may have been taken at the award ceremony for his Silver Star for the April 12 mission.

The month of May 1943 brought bad weather and few missions. A number of the men were finishing their tours and due to rotate back to the United States. The Weekly Status and Operations Report kept requesting more flight crews, especially copilots. The personnel, ground and air, were stretched thin. Morale problems among the ground crews were noted due to the lack of leave time and the wear and tear of jungle combat. Fresh food was rare early in 1943, so General Kenney personally intervened to rectify the problem:

> I finally had a showdown on the food situation. After trying all the legal means that I knew to get the rations in New Guinea improved, without any luck, I ordered fresh meat and vegetables flown to Australia . . . so the kids could have fresh food oftener than once every ten days. . . . my doctors were beginning to get worried about scurvy.[106]

Delmar wrote to his little sister Carrie Lee in early May, and with the food situation improving, he obviously had time to devote his thoughts to other, more important matters. He sent his sister and confidante (and matchmaker?) this note:

Miss Carrie Lee Dotson
Memorial Hall Nurse's Home
Richmond, Virginia

T/Sgt. Delmar Dotson
65th Sq. 43rd Bomb Gp (H)
A.P.O. 929 San Francisco, Calif.

May 9, 1943

Hello "Sis,"

I'm sending you $1,100.00 for Mother. You take $50 give her the rest. Don't you spend it on a technician [?] or I'll kick the heck out of him. You do have one don't you?

Yes, I'll take that blond. Buy me one if possible. Be sure she has some oof oof oof oof oof.

Sure wish I would hurry and get relieved out of this place, it don't get a bit better here. All you do here is dream of women.

Delmar

As living conditions in New Guinea slowly improved, entertainment started to become a part of life on the base. General Kenney loved the world premiere of the play *Hells a Papuan* staged right outside his headquarters. The "kids," as he called them, had written the play and practiced for weeks with the coaching of some of the Red Cross girls. He noted that the orchestra was made up of name-band players (maybe Delmar even snuck in the trumpet section), and the orchestra leader did a fine job, when he was not fulfilling his P-38 mechanic's duties.[107]

Even this couldn't keep Delmar's mind off of home. On May 30, 1943, Delmar wrote Carrie again and said, "Sis, between you and I your brother is going bush happy. And he is also getting darn tired of this place. I want to be in Richmond loving some of your nurse friends. You had better have me a couple on ice when I get back, O.K.?"

NIGHT FIGHTERS

Listen Here, Tojo! flew on the night of June 25 to bomb the Japanese airfield of Vunakanau near Rabaul. This time, Walter Brenneman was at the controls of #552. Walter's copilot for this mission was Lt. William Wilson, a Texan come to the Southwest Pacific to give the Japs what for. They took off with eleven other planes at 4:00 p.m. and landed at the forward staging airfield of Dobadura an hour later. They left Dobadura just after midnight, about 12:30 a.m., and immediately hit horrific weather. Continuing the mission, Brenneman found the skies clear over the target. The planes arrived at their target at 3:20 a.m. and dropped their bombs on the fuel and ammo dumps. In addition to seeing explosions at the dumps, they also observed damage to some of the parked airplanes. Antiaircraft was very heavy and not accurate, but a worse fate was waiting for them. Lurking in the skies, waiting for his moment to attack, was Superior Flight Petty Officer Shigetoshi Kudo. He was flying a specially equipped night fighter, a Nakajima J1N1 "Irving." He swooped down on #552 from above, but Brenneman and *Listen Here,*

Tojo! evaded him. Kudo continued his assault on the formation of B-17s, and he subsequently shot down two bombers of the raiding party.[108]

At this point in the war, the Japanese victories were becoming few and far between. One Japanese soldier recorded his despair in his diary, later captured and translated:

> April 22 (Hollandia) The daily air raids give the illusion that the world will burst open . . . dead bodies scattered about. . . . Can we not keep these detestable Americans at a respectful distance? It is indeed a pitiful situation. . . . Bullets and cannon shells are falling . . . about 200 enemy aircraft are persistently making strafing attacks. . . . Resigned to death, I entered the muddy jungle.
>
> May 2—How can our force recapture the lost territory? I suppose I shall fade into the dust of New Guinea. . . . I am now nothing but skin and bones . . . harassed by malaria. . . . Even if this is war, to live out the days in this suffering is a waste of life.
>
> May 24—In the valley everywhere I hear the devils firing. . . . today the enemy aircraft are again flying in formation. . . . As I again looked toward the sea, I could see the huge enemy fleet. . . . This is my last appeal.[109]

Walter Brenneman was typical of the veteran pilots of the 43rd who had put the Japanese on the run. He had won a Silver Star the same day as Delmar, flying in a later mission. Brenneman also knew five-foot-tall ball gunner Arthur Jingozian well. Jingozian, famous for personally kicking the bombs out of the bomb bay, wanted to buy Brenneman's motorcycle. Brenneman couldn't keep it running and sold it for $50.00. Jingozian fixed it up and resold it for $100.00 to a master sergeant in ordinance.[110] Brenneman would not have minded Jingozian's profit; a pilot liked to keep his gunners happy.

On July 3, Delmar, concerned there would be no women left for him to date once he returned stateside in a few months, wrote little sister Carrie Lee again, "Hey, if you have a couple of girls (<u>nurses preferred</u>) let them know I'll give them a break when I get home. Here's a couple of letters from two friends of mine. O.K., yes, and photos of Gloria. You're still my best girlfriend besides Mother. Love, Delmar."

One of the pictures Delmar sent home. The plane is 124537 Talisman of the 63rd Squadron. This plane would later become the personal airplane of Maj. Gen. J. L. Frink, Supply.[III]

At some point, Delmar would have learned, from Carrie Lee most likely, that his grandfather Old Wib Branham had died in January of 1943. The loss of one of the few father figures in his life would have added to his woes since he missed attending the funeral. Wib was laid to rest on a hill overlooking Pound, Virginia, as if watching over his brood one last time. One of Wib's earliest memories had been burying his father during the American Civil War. One of his last memories was to watch his grandsons march off to fight to the death in a World War.

Hal Winfrey was back at the controls of *Listen Here, Tojo!* in July. He flew #552 on the 25th of the month to attack Salamua on the north coast of New Guinea, but the mission was cancelled due to bad weather over the target. On the 29th Winfrey took #552 out again, this time loaded with ten five hundred-pound bombs. Something malfunctioned and Winfrey found himself barreling down the runway in *Listen Here, Tojo!* with a belly full of bombs. Visions of the McCullar disaster in April may

Wib Branham born 1858 Pound, VA, died January 1943 Pound, VA

have crossed his mind. Winfrey made a decision to ground loop (spin the plane around) to stop it from colliding with the trees along side of the runway. The wheel assemblies and the bottom of the fuselage were heavily damaged, and it would be weeks before #552 could fly again.[112]

41-24552 Listen Here, Tojo! *USAF. Though unconfirmed, Delmar's sister Carrie Lee believed that Delmar is in the front window of #552 in this picture.*

AUGUST 1943

The Southwest Pacific war was changing. The Allies were on the path to victory, not yet certain, but more and more apparent. MacArthur and his Australian/American infantry were pushing the Japanese out of all the parts of New Guinea that mattered. The veteran crews, like the one of Walter Brenneman, lost on August 4, were being missed. The B-17s were now being phased out in favor of the longer-ranged B-24s. Crews were already transitioning to the new aircraft. Delmar sent home a photo of himself in the crew of a B-24 bomber.

Back in his familiar B-17 for the moment, Delmar was assigned to the crew of Hank Dyminski on B-17 #41-24548, possibly the same plane he was on when he won his Silver Star, the "San Antonio Rose." This may be the mission to bomb Salamua on August 9 mentioned in unit reports. The bombers on this mission were using five hundred-pound M-124 bombs with delayed fuses, in this case set to detonate two hours after making landfall. The weapons of war were growing in sophistication. The flak was light and five hits were observed.

Dotson, front right with pistol on hip. The plane is a B-24D Liberator from the 531st Squadron, 380th Bomb Group #42-40522 Deliverer. The plane arrived in the Southwest Pacific May 5, 1943. Other crewmembers are unknown, but Lt. David Brennan flew the plane starting in July 1943.

THEY DON'T LIVE TOO LONG

On the 18th of August, Delmar had to fill in with another crew because one of his fellow flight engineers, Bill Walker, couldn't fly that day. On the 21st Delmar flew with Lt. Eberly, possibly on B-17 #472 *Guinea Pig*. The 43rd Bomb Group's Weekly Status Reports noted that it was difficult to maintain the needed operational tempo due to hospitalizations and combat fatigue. Tired crews were flying tired airplanes. General Kenney had been upset when he found out that medals awarded for bravery would be replaced by "ribbons only" for the duration of the war. The decision to make this change was intended to save the valuable metal used in the production of the decorations. Kenney felt that any boost to the men's spirits at this point in the war was essential to keep up the flagging morale of the New Guinea combatants. In writing Donald Nelson of the War Production Board, he confided: "I feel quite strongly about the matter, for these youngsters of mine don't live too long at best in this game."[113]

Rumors swirled in September that more men were going home soon. Australian infantry moved along the northern coast of New Guinea and made headway against the entrenched Japanese. It was no time to slow down operations and allow the enemy to regroup, so crews were patched together and sent out to keep up the pressure. The men could sense that victory in New Guinea was near.

In the ready room when the squadron assignments were made, Delmar found that his September 15th flight would be made with a veteran crew. Howard Eberly, the pilot who had swam fourteen hours to escape a crash months earlier, had over thirty completed combat missions. Charles Ranker would be the copilot. One new man assigned to the crew that day, navigator 2nd Lt. George Stacy, had been with the unit only a few short weeks and had completed four missions. The mission was to be a short one, on the north coast of New Guinea, so the new man was likely not a concern. Delmar was one of the old men of the unit by now as flight engineer. Arthur Jingozian, the five-foot-tall bomb bay acrobat, manned the ball turret. Lt. Edgar Townsend, bombardier, rounded out the officers. Gunners Joseph Ferraiolo (Silver Star) and Jennings Messer (Air Medal) would handle any Japs who strayed along. Watson Hall and tail gunner Peter Owens made up the rest of the crew.

That day's mission was to climb over the Owen Stanley Mountains, make the run to Lae, and bomb the Japs, pretty straightforward. Australian ground forces were closing in on the town, so the men were told to make sure they got their bombs on target. With this crew, a good bomb run shouldn't have been a problem. Delmar would have been involved with the preflight checks and may have taken more time than normal. On this day, they were assigned to old #552 *Listen Here, Tojo!*, recently repaired and now ready for action. The ground crew turned over the props. Ground crews rotated the propellers to pulled fuel into the cylinders and prepared the engine for startup—they counted "9 blades" to know they had turned the engines enough. Lt. Eberly started the engines, and he and his copilot and Delmar listened to the familiar whine of smooth-running engines. Eberly pushed the throttles forward, and *Listen Here, Tojo!*, laden with bombs, roared down the runway. Pulling back on the stick, Eberly lifted her off and freed her of the dirty humidity that plagued the mortals below. Eberly and #552 climbed for altitude to prepare to cross the formidable mountains. The *Listen Here, Tojo!* had a date to keep.

Chapter Nine:

CLOUDS

WEDNESDAY, SEPTEMBER 15, 1943

As the crew of *Listen Here, Tojo!* traveled toward the Owen Stanley Mountains between 8 and 9 a.m., they fell into their military routines and private superstitions. Lt. Crawford, whom Delmar had flown with on the April 12th Silver-Star mission, always wore his lucky hat. No doubt today's crew had similar talismans to ward off the evil that awaited them. Even after a year in the Southwest Pacific, everyone took their work seriously. Only a few weeks before, *Georgia Peach* and Lt. Walter Brenneman had been lost to Jap fighters. Sgt. Major Katsuiaki Kira and the 24th Sentai (air group) were in the area. Kira would have twenty-one kills during the war (he survived) and may have been the one who killed Brenneman and the guys August 3. Their Nakajima Type II fighters were called "Oscars," an army version of the more famous Japanese Navy "Zero" fighters. With fighters swirling around her, *Georgia Peach* had gone down until she hit the sea. No chutes had come out, and the plane had sunk immediately.[114] The #552 and her crew readied for action.

THE PLANE

The #552, her undercarriage repaired for this mission, sported her now famous nose art and *Listen Here, Tojo!* name. She also carried the painted bomb icons indicating that she had flown seventy-seven missions and had sunk numerous ships. She was not flying alone today, as her sisters rose with her to go to war one more time. The #552 had been one of the last B-17s delivered to the 5th Air Force, as the B-24 was now supplanting her in the 63rd, 64th, and 65th Squadrons of the 43rd. The European Theater still got priority, and the demand for B-17s there was great. Besides, the B-24s had longer range and could carry more bombs, which was a needed improvement flying over the vast expanses of the Pacific. The formation of twelve B-17 bombers constituted a large formation by Southwest Pacific standards and that day would be one of the last B-17 raids in the Pacific War.

THE CREW

First Lt. Howard Eberly from Portland, Oregon, may have been glad today's mission was mostly over land. It had been exactly six months to the day since he went down over water. On March 15, Eberly had been the copilot with 1st Lt. Arthur McMullan on the B-17 *Hell From Heaven Men* 41-24424. Eberly's plane had run out of fuel and ditched at sea. Even though the B-17 was considered one of the better planes to be in if you had to hit the water, only copilot Eberly, bombardier 2nd Lt. John Dawson, and radioman S/Sgt. Freeman survived the landing. Eberly crawled out of the copilot's window and went into the water. Not being able to find the plane's life raft, the three men started the fifteen-mile swim to shore. An additional voice was heard calling out, but Eberly, Dawson, and Freeman could not locate him, and the voice did not call again. After swimming all night, they were within five miles of land. The tide began to pull the three away from land, and Freeman decided not to fight but to drift on the tide. He was never heard from again, and his family back in Arkansas only knew that he was missing in action. Lts. Eberly and Dawson survived the fourteen-hour swim in the shark-infested waters and eventually made their way back to the 43rd.[115]

Today it would be 2nd Lt. Edgar Townsend from Bronxville, New York, flying beside Eberly as his copilot. Townsend, only nineteen years of age, was on only his second combat mission. He had originally been trained to fly A-20 twin-engine bombers, but because of a copilot shortage, he was transferred to the four-engine B-17s while the unit prepared to transition to B-24s. He had only been in the unit six weeks at the time of the mission.

The navigator, 2nd Lt. George Stacy from Erie, Pennsylvania, was a relative newcomer with just four missions under his belt. George Stacy, like Delmar Dotson, had been a prewar army man, also serving in Hawaii. He had enlisted in the Army Air Corps in 1938 and later went to flight school and Officer Candidate School. He had just written his mother that he had forty-six missions to go before he returned home.

Lt. Howard Eberly, second from left

Second Lt. Charles Ranker of Tiffin, Ohio, was the bombardier on the mission. He was proud of his graduation from Bombardier School and wore his class ring on combat missions. Gunners S/Sgt. Theodore McCartney from Bellevue, Pennsylvania, and S/Sgt. Watson Hall from Abbeville, South Carolina, were assigned to the crew that day as well. McCartney, remembered as a "gung-ho gutsy guy," originally wanted to be a paratrooper but was too light. He asked what the next most dangerous job was and eventually became a gunner. Without a father in the home before the war, Ted had helped provide for his mother and his six brothers and sister.[116]

Lieutenant George L. Stacy

Watson C. Hall

Hall had enlisted on October 26, 1942, and sailed for Australia June 3, 1943.[117]

Radioman S/Sgt. Joseph Ferraialo from East Haven, Connecticut, knew the damage the enemy fighters could do on the attack. He was a holder of the Distinguished Flying Cross for his actions on March 8, 1943. While he was a part of the crew of *This Old Man*, B-17F 41-24403, his plane was on a solo reconnaissance mission when a formation of Zeros swarmed the lone plane. The pilot, copilot, bombardier, and navigator were all wounded, but the injured crew fought off the Japanese and made a landing at Dobadura.

Jennings Messer from Williamson, West Virginia, and by now a sergeant, owned a Silver Star for gallantry over Rabaul on February 2, 1943, and an Air Medal for his actions on a mission to Kavieng on April 2, 1943. Along with his gunnery responsibilities, today he was serving as the assistant flight engineer.

Sgt. Jennings Messer, top right. USAF

Sgt. Arthur Jingozian from East Bridgewater, Massachusetts, was strapped in his ball turret on January 24, 1943, when his pilot, Lt. Vernon Strawser, caught it in the chest and fell forward, mortally wounded, on the controls. As the copilot and flight engineer tried to pull him off of the controls, the plane plunged from 22,000 feet to 8,000 feet. Finally bringing the plane under control, the copilot landed at Dobadura with one engine out and another running roughly. Between that mission and his bomb-bay ballet, Sgt. Jingozian had about seen it all.

T/Sgt. Peter Owens of Ransen, New York, manned the tail gun position. At 5'5" and 128 pounds, he could fit into the cramped position in the tail of the aircraft, manning the twin fifty calibers. After growing up in Utica, New York, he graduated from Union College in Schenectady, New York. He joined up after Pearl Harbor and eventually was assigned to the Southwest Pacific Theater and the 43rd Bomb Group.[118]

Tail gunner Peter Owens (center) in Australia

THE LAST B-17

Along with Eberly and crew, five other B-17s from the 65th Squadron and another six from the 63rd were on their way to bomb the Chinatown area of Lae on the northern New Guinea coast. The formation arrived over the target between 10:20 and 10:41 a.m. and did what they had done many times before. The antiaircraft fire rated as medium to heavy today, and cloud cover over the target added to the challenge. One B-17 was hit by flak, and three B-17s of the 63rd Squadron didn't drop on the target because the haze and clouds made them unable to confirm the target. With Australian ground forces almost surrounding the town, even at its outskirts, this was considered a wise decision. The ordinance for today's mission consisted of one thousand-pound bombs instead of the more common five hundred-pounders. Nine of the twelve B-17s dropped their bombs and scored hits on an antiair position west of the target, and one building was seen to erupt in a large explosion.

Lae Airfield after an earlier air raid 1943. USAF

With the mission completed, the planes turned for home. As the antiaircraft fire receded into the distance, the worry now was enemy fighter attacks. With no fighters apparently intercepting on this day, the next part of the mission was to gain altitude to cross over the Owen Stanley Range. Closing on the mountains, the appearance of clouds on the horizon bode ominously. A large thunder head had formed right by the pass the formation had planned to take through the mountains. This storm meant that low visibility and turbulence were about to become a serious issue.

Eberly flew the left wing position in the second echelon of the formation at about 11,500 feet on a heading of 190 degrees. Just as the B-17s entered the clouds, *Listen Here, Tojo!* immediately pulled up and to the left. Immediately, the clouds obscured what came next. Thirty seconds later the formation exited the clouds and one plane was missing—#552. Efforts were made to raise the crew of *Listen Here, Tojo!*

on the radio but to no avail. Eberly and crew just vanished. No radio message. No sighting. Nothing.

Returning to base, the remaining crews reported to their mission debriefing and reported the vanishing of the *Listen Here, Tojo!*. A B-17 was readied and a search for the #552 and her crew commenced, but after four hours the search plane returned without seeing anything. A search plane the next day, Tuesday, September 16, reported seeing a flash of light or a reflection in the area *Listen Here, Tojo!* was last seen, but when they circled back, no further light was seen. The city of Lae, last target of the *Listen Here, Tojo!*, fell to the Australians that same day.

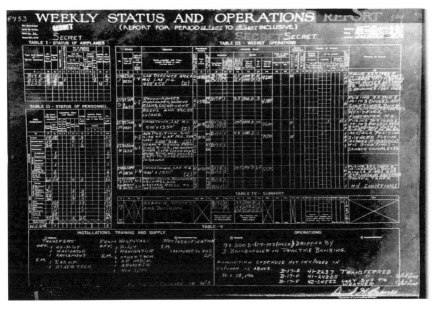

The Weekly Report for the day Listen Here, Tojo! *was lost*

In one of the reports of the disappearance, attributed to "adverse weather," a chronicler wrote of the pilot, Lt. Eberly,

> During this period, Lt. Eberly underwent an almost unendurable ordeal while on a combat mission; was evacuated, and spent two months in a hospital; returned, on his own request, to his organization; and, at the first opportunity, returned to combat flying.

From June 28, 1943, the date of Lt. Eberly's return to flying, to September 15, 1943, the date on which Lt. Eberly was listed as missing in action, he flew practically every mission this squadron had, and made every effort to have himself scheduled for the few he missed.[119]

Years later, Max Osborn of the 65th Squadron would recount the effect of casualties on the remaining men of the 43rd during the Port Moresby days. Whenever casualties occurred, a supply sergeant would come and collect the belongings of the missing man. In this case, an entire crew had disappeared. Osborn may have flown with Delmar Dotson on at least one mission with Hank Dyminski as pilot. Though the years had dimmed his memories, he remembered the empty tent next door after the crew just disappeared one September day.[120]

Lt. Howard Eberly

Chapter Ten:

THE WAR GOES ON

At 4:24 p.m. September 15, 1943, Lt. John Gibbs took off in a B-17 to search for the *Listen Here, Tojo!* and her crew. In his report of the search, he mentioned that a stationary light resembling a white flare or Very light was sighted and burned for less than a minute. The searchers also reported seeing a mirror flash or possibly even a muzzle flash. No wreckage was sighted and they returned to Port Moresby. The next morning Lt. Gibbs took off at 8:40 a.m. and searched the Wau Valley but saw nothing on this mission and returned to base.

MISSING IN ACTION (MIA)

The highly decorated crew of the *Listen Here, Tojo!* was declared missing, but the presumption was that they were dead:

1st Lt. Howard G. Eberly, Jr., pilot; Silver Star, Legion of Merit, Air Medal
2nd Lt. Edgar L. Townsend, Jr., copilot
2nd Lt. George L. Stacy, navigator
2nd Lt. Charles E. Ranker, bombardier
Tech. Sgt. Delmar Dotson, flight engineer; Silver Star American Defense Service Medal, Asiatic-Pacific Campaign Medal
Sgt. Jennings Messer, asst. flight engineer; Silver Star, Air Medal
Staff Sgt. Joseph Ferraiolo, radio; Distinguished Flying Cross
Staff Sgt. Theodore J. McCartney, gunner; Air Medal

Staff Sgt. Watson C. Hall, gunner; Air Medal, Asiatic-Pacific
  Campaign Medal, Aerial Gunner's Badge
Sgt. Arthur Jingozian, ball turret gunner; Air Medal with three
  oak leaf clusters, Distinguished Flying Cross
Tech. Sgt. Peter Owens, tail gunner/photographer

It was always possible for someone to walk out of that impenetrable jungle, but it was not very likely. The proper forms were filled out, and the men's personal effects prepared for the shipment home. Word of the disaster was slow to reach the family. Delmar's mother was notified in Pound, Virginia, on September 22, 1943, but few details were forthcoming due to "reasons of military security." Little sister Carrie Lee was reading the Sunday, October 10, *Richmond Times-Dispatch* when, to her horror, she saw Delmar's name listed among the missing-in-action. Then, to her dismay, the last letter she had written Delmar was returned to her marked, "Missing in Action." The light went out of her world to think that her protector was no longer out there. The letter she wrote that Delmar never read:

September 5, 1943
Dearest Brother,

Received your letters and the pictures. They were numbered one through sixteen and all except #11 was here. What happened to number eleven, did you forget and snap a Jap? By the way all the girls here are calling you their hero.

Though I didn't see it they say there was a write-up in the Times about you and some other guys being honored for a flight over Jap bases last April. I don't know what it was all about except we all were thrilled to death about you and you headed the list. I want to get a clipping and send it to Mom—she'll probably celebrate and invite the President to dinner!

Glenn and I teased her about the big pictures of you and he she had all over the house. She had a big picture of you on the mantel and sitting beside a big one of General MacArthur and Glenn says she thinks you are the General and he you!

Ralph is in California so he might be a member of the South Pacific front someday, too.

Who is this Gloria? She sure is an attractive "little girl."

Mrs. Turner is the one who called me and told me about that silver star honorship (or whatever it was) and she and "Pop" [Delmar's football coach] were as excited as if you yourself had won the war, already!

Seems strange that as I sit here writing you the radio is playing a story of flyers in New Guinea—the incident very familiar to yours. Makes you feel sorta funny.

Well, hero, if you were here now the girls would all tear you apart trying to get a portion of you (and not because of meat rationing either). Be good, take care of yourself and write soon.

Love,
Sis

[stamped] RETURN TO WRITER UNCLAIMED, Missing in Action

The bad news continued to arrive for the Dotson family. Chaplain Thomas Shea wrote Delmar's mother, Delsie, in October and told her:

In my Chaplain's experience in the Air Force of more than two years I have observed no one who got along better with his fellows that T/Sgt Dotson. All liked him. His cheery, fun-loving ways were ever a good influence amidst the strains of combat.

At present we know nothing of what happened after his plane left the flight entering a cloud bank. As we move northward something may be learned definitely. . . . I pray that God will lessen your uneasiness of mind by resignation to His Will and His Protecting Providence. I have remembered Delmar at Mass and will continue to do so.

Thos. F. Shea
Major C.C. Group Chaplain

The Move Northward

In his letter to Delmar's mother, Chaplain Shea wrote what everyone was sensing: the 43rd was about to move north. With ground forces advancing, it was time for the 43rd to move out as well. In December, the 43rd Bomb Group moved to Dobadura, New Guinea, and established its base of operations there. A little over ten weeks after that, the sons of the 43rd moved again and began operations out of Nadzab, New Guinea. By July 1944, the 43rd was on the move forward yet again, this time to Owi, Schouten Islands, New Guinea. The rising Allied tide meant that the airbases needed to be moved forward to support the advances of the armies and the navies.

In November 1944, the planes and crews of the 43rd Bombardment Group (Heavy) moved to the Philippine islands. Not since the early days of the war when the 19th Bomb Group had begun the long retreat, had Allied bombers struck at the Japanese from the Philippine Islands.

Even with the logistical challenges of constantly relocating a heavy bomber unit, the accommodations of the men had improved immensely. Lt. George Hunter of the 63rd Squadron, 43rd, would receive teasing letters from his wife instructing him not to write her anymore about his unit volleyball team losing games. It should be noted that among Lt. Hunter's keepsakes from the war was the groups' volleyball schedule. Hunter's 63rd Squadron team opened league play versus the Headquarters team.[121]

As the war between the United States and Japan entered 1945, the industrial might of the United States proved decisive. More men, now better trained and better equipped, arrived in ever-increasing numbers, prepared to face down the Empire of Japan and finish what had started at Pearl Harbor. The 43rd Bombardment Group, now entirely equipped with B-24 Liberator bombers, received the new men into her ranks to carry on the tradition of victory that the New Guinea men started.

THE FINISHERS—1945

Delmar's death did not end the war for the Dotson family. Little brother Ralph Dotson, now out of the Masonic Home of Virginia, was in the army. When little sister Carrie Lee told Delmar that Ralph might end up in the Pacific, she was prescient. He shipped out and spent the rest of the war scouring Pacific battlefields for the dead. His Grave's Registration unit moved from battlefield to battlefield, island to island, caring for the fallen. The task of locating hastily buried remains was so difficult that in New Guinea some frontline American graves were marked with fifteen-foot-high crosses so that the rapid jungle growth would not cover the temporary grave and it be lost. Ralph's experiences so scarred him that he would not speak of them the rest of his life. Older brother Glenn Dotson made a career out of the army but spent the war training artillerymen stateside.

Little sister Carrie Lee left the Masonic Home for nursing school. After graduation she became an army nurse and shipped out for Okinawa. Now Lt. Carrie Lee Dotson, she met a young army attorney named Gaylord Nelson, which would have great implications for her future. She finished the war on Okinawa serving at the 9th General Hospital before returning home to Pound, Virginia. By the end of the war, brother Willie was back in the army as well.

America sent her sons and daughters to fight around the world by the hundreds of thousands. The Dotson family was just one example, with two sons and one daughter in the Pacific and two sons serving stateside. Delsie Dotson had become a five-star mother and with Delmar's reported death, a Gold Star mother. Delmar and others had stemmed the Japanese advances in the Pacific, and now more help was on the way. With victory in Europe finally achieved, the Pacific, at last, became the nation's priority.

IDA, LOUISIANA

A small-town boy from a large family, Gray Allison was born May 7, 1924. He was the eighth of ten children born to Buddy and Ora Allison in the town of Ida, Louisiana. Called "Boo" within the family, Gray grew up in a loving home and prospered in every opportunity given him, from scouting to sports. December 7, 1941, was a day of tragedy for Gray and the Allison family but not just because of Pearl Harbor. His father, Buddy Allison, had been killed in a tragic accident, and Buddy's funeral was on that fateful Sunday, Pearl Harbor Day.[122]

After some time in the Army Air Force Reserve, Gray Allison was called up for Air Force active duty in February 1943. While in flight training, one of the psychologists wanted him to discuss in detail the death of his father. When Allison refused, the doctor threatened to have him dropped from pilot training. With the stubborn, principled ideals that became such a hallmark of his life, he went to see another psychologist and got restored to pilot training. Training completed, he learned he was going to the South Pacific with the 43rd Bombardment Group, 65th Squadron, flying B-24s against the Empire of Japan.

That the small town boys of the American nation would confidently go off to fight a war against a genocidal enemy expecting to win is a testament to the American character and ethos. Once in the Pacific Theater, Lt. Allison soon adopted the look of a confident pilot. Commanding an airplane crew at the age of twenty, he looked the part. Leather jacket with "Louisiana Lady" painted on the back, a silk scarf, and a cigar completed the outfit. In other words, he fit right in. Known for his steely blue eyes and penetrating stare, one person would remark later in his life, "When Gray Allison looked at you, you stayed looked at."

Before they were to fly out of San Francisco and off to war, Allison told his crew they should go out for a fancy dinner their last night stateside since, after all, they might not be coming back. He chose the Top of the Mark Restaurant, and when they arrived, the maître d' checked their identification. At that time, California law prohibited anyone under twenty-one going into a restaurant that served alcohol. When it was discovered that Lt. Allison was only twenty, he was denied entry, even though he didn't drink. He spent his last night in the United

States waiting outside while his crew enjoyed their meal. Afterward they laughingly nicknamed him "Baby" for his youthfulness.

By the time Lt. Allison arrived with the 65th Squadron of the 43rd Bomb Group, the squadron's nickname had become "The Lucky Dicers." Their logo was a picture of two dice on the tail planes of the B-24s. On one side of the plane, the dice showed the numbers "6" and "5" (for 65th Squadron), and on the other side of the plane, the dice showed "4" and "3" (for 43rd Bomb Group).

Insignia of the 65th Squadron during the B-24 era (by Jeremy Clark)

Allison's copilot, 2nd Lt. Owen Ernsthausen, had recorded the journey he and Allison made to get to the 65th Squadron and the war, and it read like a history of the war in the Pacific, showing how far the Allies had advanced since the New Guinea days. Lt. Ernsthausen's records show that the crew flew B-24 44-50785 on the trip across the Pacific:

April 6—Flew from Mather Field, California, to John Rodgers, Honolulu
April 8—Flew from John Rodgers to Christmas Island
April 9—Flew from Christmas Island to Canton Island
April 10—Flew from Canton Island to Tarawa Island
April 11—Flew from Tarawa Island to Guadalcanal Island
April 12—Flew from Guadalcanal Island to Biak Island[123]

On May 1 Ernsthausen, nicknamed "Ernie" by his crewmates, recorded their first combat mission. Flying out of Nadzab, New Guinea, in a B-24J, they bombed Wewak, a target Delmar Dotson and the *Listen Here, Tojo!* would have known well. The B-24s and Lt. Allison's crew pounded Wewak for days. From May 1 to May 7 they hit the area four times (May 1, 4, 6, 7). On the 26th they flew their first mission to Rabaul. The Japanese base at Rabaul had been bypassed by the Allies in their island-hopping strategy. It was now left to "die on the vine" as the vernacular of the day put it. However, even cut off and isolated, Rabaul still represented a formidable threat.

Unit Sign Painted on the Wing of an Enemy Airplane, Clark Field USAF

RETURN TO THE PHILIPPINES

By June, Lt. Allison and crew flew out of Clark Field in the Philippines. The dangers of war were ever present. In May, pilot Jim Cherkauer and his B-24J *Pretty Gal* crew barely survived after making an emergency landing with two engines out. On the bomb run, the B-24 next to them exploded in mid-air, peppering their aircraft with shrapnel. As if this wasn't enough, they were also hit with Jap antiaircraft fire. In June, Frank Chisman on board the B-24 *Barbara Jean* crashed after takeoff, and everyone on board was killed.

Matt Holohan of the 64th Squadron remembered his first time to fly into Clark Field. He was one of the first bombers to arrive, and he found out that the Control Tower was "a fighter at the end of the runway." While taxiing off the runway, his nose wheel got stuck in a soft spot and turned sideways. A steamroller parked next to the strip made it impossible to get his plane unstuck, so he left the pilot's seat and drove the steamroller out of the way, narrowly missing the red pennants that he thought marked a new construction site. He then returned to his plane and taxied it to its parking area. After he got out of the plane, someone informed him that the red pennants marked uncleared Japanese land mines.[124]

THE JUNE 13 MISSION

In his later life, the now Dr. Gray Allison spoke to a ladies group and mentioned that he would soon be travelling to Hong Kong. One of the ladies in the meeting spoke up and asked in her deep Southern drawl—a mixture of humidity and molasses—"Dr. Allison, have you ever been to Hong Kong before?" Allison, always known for his concise answers said, "Yes, ma'am." To which she immediately followed up with, "Oh, what did you do when you were there?" "I bombed it," he responded.

The Japanese had been using wooden sampans to gather intelligence, and many of them harbored in the port of Hong Kong. Allison and his crew were chosen to fly a mission with an experimental munition to rid the harbor of these boats. Ernsthausen's log noted that they were with the 45th Squadron Experimental for the mission. Lt. Allison recounted that fifty-five-gallon drums were filled with a combustible mixture of jellied gasoline called Napalm and then grenades attached to the tops of the drums. The idea was that the drums would burst open upon contact with the water, the fuel mixture would spread out on top of the water, and then the grenades would ignite the mixture and burn out the sampans. Also, they would have to fly low and slow over the target, and the crew would have to pull the pins on the grenades just before they shoved out the drums of Napalm.

Lt. Allison and the B-24 made their approach, dropped to altitude, and pulled back on the throttles. They were now flying just above the water at slow speed, right on top of the Jap position. Once the pins were pulled, the clock was ticking, so the drums were pushed out of the plane in good order. However, instead of the drums spilling their contents to spread out on the harbor's surface, they immediately plunged to the depths. They sank so fast that the crew didn't even hear the detonation of the grenades. Mission over; back to base.

General George Kenney described another mission in March 1945 using the new weapon of Napalm or, as he called it, "liquid gasoline."

> Seven B-24s had made the 2400-mile round-trip flight from Morotai to Soerabaya. One of them came in at 15,000-feet altitude to attract the Jap searchlights and antiaircraft guns and two others, flying about two miles apart, synchronized their arrival over the target at the 6000-foot level with that of the first B-24 to further confuse the Japanese. About two minutes behind these three decoys, flying just above the water, came the other four bombers, which skip-bombed the docks with fifty-gallon drums of Napalm, the jellied gasoline incendiary that we had used so successfully in Leyte and Luzon.[125]

After several more missions from Clark Field, the 65th Squadron and the rest of the 43rd Bomb Group were notified that they were moving out again, this time to the very doorstep of Japan. Key parts of their base at Clark were to be immediately disassembled and the men transported by boat to their new home. Though they didn't know at the time, the men of the 43rd were making their last move of the war.

Lt. Gray Allison, pilot, (back row, second from left) and his crew. Copilot Lt. Ernsthausen is on the back row left.

IE SHIMA

As a part of the Okinawa Campaign, the American 77th Infantry Division assaulted the nearby island of Ie Shima. The small island, only about nine square miles in size, was quickly captured and declared secure on April 24, 1945. Engineers immediately went to work removing the large number of mines, repairing the Japanese airfields, and expanding the facility. By July, the 43rd Bombardment Group was on its way to its new base just off of the island of Okinawa. Allison was told to pack up and go to Ie Shima before the rest of his crew. Years later he remembered:

> I went from Clark Field on Luzon, P.I. by plane to Ie Shima. My crew came later by boat. The 43rd had lost some pilots over Japan and flew several of us to Ie [Shima]. I flew three missions over Japan with other crews while my crew was on the way.

When the crew reunited with Lt. Allison, they complained about how bad they had it on the boat until he reminded them that he had been flying combat missions while they were sailing across the Pacific. Ie Shima became a major staging area with the transfer of the 43rd Bomb Group in July. In addition to the 43rd, the 419th Night Fighter Squadron, XIII Fighter Command, 421st Night Fighter Squadron (flying P-61s), and squadrons of the 38th Bombardment Group (Heavy) also relocated there. One pilot later called Ie Shima a "land-based aircraft carrier" since one airstrip extended across the entire side of the island. In addition to water all around, the pilots had to fly directly over a sheer cliff just before landing.[126]

Ie Shima as seen from the air, late WWII
(Artistic rendering by Jeremy Clark)

In the lulls between missions, the crews took advantage of the down time. The US Air Force made it a point to provide leisurely activities for the men whenever possible. The ever-present volleyball teams reformed, and league play resumed. Some of Allison's crew discovered during this time that they were apparently "seriously malnourished," considering the luxuries that some of the US Navy and Navy Sea Bees were enjoying. Finding out that cans of peaches were on the island, a plan was hatched to liberate the aforesaid items. Even more distressing was the revelation that certain branches of the service had ice makers, of all things. Being the military men that they were, a plan was formulated, and soon the crew was enjoying peach ice cream. The only distraction from the moment of delight was the disruption caused by certain persons of other branches of the service looking for some missing items.

Also during this time, a typhoon struck the island of Ie Shima. Lt. Allison remembered spending the night with his arms wrapped around a stake in the ground as the gale force winds blew his tent away. Several aircraft were moved into the water by the force of the storm across the airfields of Ie Shima.

About the weather, Allison remembered:

> They gave us weather classes when we were in training. We studied days on end about weather. We went to the Pacific in New Guinea and they were still teaching us weather classes while we were flying out of there. We lost more airplanes in the Pacific during World War II to weather than we did to Japanese antiaircraft and aircraft combined. The weather is something in the South Pacific—huge thunderstorms we called "anvil-top thunderstorms" because they looked like an anvil on top. Some of them were 50,000 feet high, and sometimes you'd see 10 to 12 of them joined together across the sky. They were terrible storms with fierce winds going up 100 to 200 m.p.h. Winds could be going down in the column right next to it, the same speed the airplane is flying and it would be torn all to pieces. We knew all about the power of those storms.

One day, as we were coming back from a bombing run in Japan, we flew into one of those storms. I had never been in weather like that in my life, and it was not even one of the really bad ones. We had to break up formation and get as far apart as we could, then I flew into one of those storms and, before I knew it, we were up 5,000 feet, then down 5,000 feet. The plane was going up and down and I had no control over it; that storm had control.[127]

Wednesday, August 8, Lt. Allison and his crew were back in action, bombing targets on the Japanese mainland. Though they weren't aware of it at the moment, two days previously the 20th Air Force had dropped the first atomic bomb on the city of Hiroshima, Japan. Meanwhile, Allied ground forces were preparing the invasion of the Japanese homelands, with some estimates predicting hundreds of thousands of Allied dead and wounded. On August 9, the second atomic bomb was dropped on the city of Nagasaki, and rumors began to swirl that something big had happened.

The stresses of war were building to a crescendo, and the pressures on the crews were intense. No one wanted to be among the last in the war to die. While in the landing pattern on final approach, Lt. Allison was cut off by the pilot of another B-24, and only his quick reflexes spared his crew from disaster. Recovering the aircraft and resuming his landing approach took time, so by the time he landed, the pilot of the offending airplane was no longer on the field. Lt. Allison, having just escaped death through the carelessness of a fellow pilot, went looking for him in a cold rage. "I was so mad that if I'd found that pilot I would have shot him. I looked everywhere; I had my .45 on my hip."

On August 11, Lt. Allison's crew bombed the Japanese port of Ibusuki at the entrance of Kagoshima Bay. The crews were flying a mission every three days, and with the scuttlebutt saying that the war in the Pacific was about to end, the crew may have believed that they had just flown their last mission. They had survived the war.

When Lt. Allison went by the Squadron Operations center, he noticed that his crew was scheduled to go out again the next day, August 12. Whether a clerical error or not, he went to the commanding officer on behalf of his crew to right this wrong. The commanding officer told

Lt. Allison that the orders would stand as written and that he and his crew would fly again tomorrow. When Lt. Allison went back and broke the news, his crew was not happy. In fact, Allison was worried himself. He got very little sleep that night thinking that he was going to die on the last mission of the war because of a scheduling error. General Kenney had written, "I never saw a flyer yet who didn't worry about this 'one last mission' business. I don't like it myself."[128] The crew arose early for their 7:30 a.m. takeoff and went about their duties. They bombed Matsuyama Airfield on the island of Formosa and returned to base. Allison liked to put a cigar in his mouth (unlit, of course, onboard the aircraft) at the end of each mission, and this was the best one yet.

SURRENDER

The long-awaited day finally arrived for the men of the 43rd Bomb Group. The news spread fast and the communiqué made it official.

> August 15, 1945
> From Supreme Commander for the Allied Powers to the Japanese Emperor, the Japanese Imperial Government, the Japanese Imperial General Headquarters
>
> Message Number Z-500
>
> I have been designated as the Supreme Commander for the Allied Powers (the United States, the Republic of China, the United Kingdom and the Union of Soviet Socialist Republics) and empowered to arrange directly with the Japanese authorities for the cessation of hostilities at the earliest practicable date.
>
> It is desired that a radio station in the Tokyo area be officially designated for continuous use in handling radio communications between this headquarters and your headquarters. Your reply to this message should give the call signs, frequencies and station designation. It is desired that the radio communication with my headquarters in Manila be handled in English text.

Pending designation by you of a station in the Tokyo area for use as above indicated, station JUM on frequency 13705 kilocycles will be used for this purpose and Manila will reply on 15965 kilocycles.

Upon receipt of this message, acknowledge.

Signed
MacArthur.[129]

The war was over. The 43rd Bomb Group had sailed from Boston to Australia in 1942 and fought its way to the home islands of Japan by 1945. The horrors of war were not yet finished for the Allison crew. They were assigned a new type of duty—ferrying released Prisoners of War (POWs). When Lt. Allison and his crew arrived back in the Philippines, they knew they were going to transport some of the Americans who had been prisoners of the Japanese. Some of these prisoners were survivors of the Bataan Death March and had been interned for the entire war. What shocked the Allison crew were the skeletons with parchment skin stretched over the bones that prepared to board their B-24. Barely able to walk, the freed POWs wept as they headed to a home they thought they would never see again.

HOMEWARD BOUND

On November 3 (his wife-to-be's nineteenth birthday), Lt. Allison started the long journey home. He flew to Clark Field, Tinian, and eventually back to the States. Lt. Allison was unable to cable ahead to let his mother know he was coming, and so when he walked in the door of the Ida, Louisiana, home, he was surprised that she had put fresh sheets on his bed and made cookies. When he asked her how she knew he was coming, she told him that she just prepared every day for his homecoming, and she knew eventually he would be home safe and sound.

Though Allison struggled with what he had seen of war, especially the condition of the American prisoners, he never struggled with what

SONS OF THE 43RD

he had done in the war. The Japanese had started the fight, and he, the men of the 43rd, and the Allied soldiers like them had finished it.

While Lt. Allison and the survivors of the war struggled to adjust to peace, Delmar Dotson's family struggled with the uncertainty of his disappearance and tried to pick up the pieces of their lives. Ralph Dotson came home from the war and tried out for the Chicago Cubs baseball team. He made the cut and pitched a few games in the minor leagues, but a lingering neck injury derailed his baseball dreams. He never married. Carrie Lee Dotson came home from Okinawa and married Gaylord Nelson, the attorney she had met in the army, and started a family.

WHERE IS MY SON?

Delsie continued to deal with the aftermath of Delmar's disappearance. The army officially declared him dead, his remains unrecoverable as of September 16, 1944, and sent his personal items home. The inventory of Delmar's worldly goods read:

1 Large tinted photograph
1 Picture frame
1 Bundle of music
1 Bible
1 Wallet
1 T-shirt
1 Bunch, beads
1 Mega mute
1 Ukelele in case
1 Ukelele without strings[130]

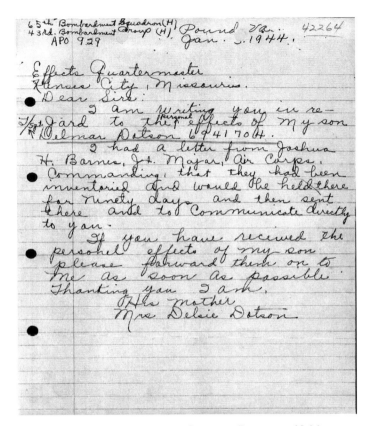

Letter from Delsie Dotson January 1944

Delmar's family still wanted to know what had happened to him and even to hold out hope that somehow he had survived the war, or at least to find some sort of closure. Older sister Laura wrote the General of the Air Force, Hap Arnold, to ask if anything could be done to learn of her brother's status. She received a detailed reply from Major General Edward Witsell. MG Witsell wrote:

> A copy of your letter of 26 August 1945, addressed to General H. H. Arnold, concerning your brother, Technical Sergeant Delmar Dotson, has been referred to this office.
>
> I am indeed sorry that so much grief has come to you, and the hope you entertain for your brother's survival is most understandable. . . .

The circumstances related [of the disappearance] were such that there was some basis for hope for Sergeant Dotson's survival at the time he disappeared, but after the lapse of twelve months these circumstances, when considered in connection with all other relevant circumstances, lost their significance. . . .

My heartfelt sympathy is with you and all other members of Sergeant Dotson's family in the great loss you have been called upon to bear.

Sincerely Yours,
Edward F. Witsell, Major General
Acting the Adjutant General of the Army

As if to further torment the family, tales of incredible survival circulated at the end of the war. After missing for months, Sergeant Gordon Manuel, a bombardier with the 64th Squadron of the 43rd Bomb Group, walked out of the jungle alive. His bomber made a night attack on Vunakanau Air Field at Rabaul on May 21, 1943. A Jap night fighter attacked their bomber, and the crew was ordered to bail out. Only the copilot and Sgt. Manuel jumped before the plane exploded. They landed in the water and made it to shore. The lieutenant was captured and executed. Manuel, with a broken leg, hid for four days by a stream, drinking the water and eating snails that he caught. He hobbled inland and met friendly natives who nursed him back to health. Speaking Pidgin English with the natives, he eventually set up a collection plan to gather other Allied crew members who bailed out over this Japanese island (Rabaul was on the northern end of the island of New Britain). He made contact with an Australian spotting station on the island, and whenever an Allied crew member bailed out over New Britain, Manuel's agents would collect them and take them to the Australian spotters, who would then radio for submarine pickup. After eight months, Manuel returned to the 43rd and was sent back to the States. He wanted to return to the Fifth Air Force after his convalescence, but since he had had malaria five times, he was deemed unfit to return to the Pacific.[131] In the mind of Delmar's family, if Sgt. Manuel could walk out of the jungle, maybe Delmar could as well.

But Delmar Dotson did not walk out of the jungle. The War Department had declared him dead, and with the war over, his memory began to fade away, except in the hearts of a faithful few. Beautifully framed photographs of Delmar in uniform remained on the mantel of numerous members of his family, but in time the memory of him, like the pictures, faded—forever young.

T.Sgt. Delmar Dotson, MIA

Chapter Eleven:

THE DISCOVERY

THE SENATOR'S WIFE

With the declaration of Victory in Japan Day, Lt. Carrie Lee Dotson had new worlds to conquer. Now back in the States with her new husband, Gaylord Nelson, she moved with him to his home state of Wisconsin so he could establish his law practice. Carrie Lee worked as a nurse and soon became a mother as well. Gaylord's entry into politics may have surprised her at first, but the couple's meteoric rise surprised no one who knew them well. Carrie Lee's determination became legendary as Gaylord captured the Wisconsin governorship, and she became the First Lady of the Great State of Wisconsin. Well noted (or notorious) for her strong opinions, she became a delight to columnists bored with the humdrum sameness of carefully crafted political image. Soon enough, Gaylord had his eye on an even bigger prize—running for the US Senate. They ran and he won.

Through the years, Carrie Lee would think about her protector and big brother Delmar. Her frequent reflections may have been due to the unresolved nature of his disappearance. She had no memory of her father, Albert, since she was so young when he died. Delmar, or the idea of Delmar, had

Senator Gaylord and Carrie Lee Nelson

Carrie Lee Nelson and Jackie Kennedy

played an important role in her life as her protector. Carrie Lee would dream of Delmar, young and strong, walking down the sidewalk in his pre-war khaki uniform and coming up to her circle of friends on the sidewalk. But he would never stop to speak with her; he just kept walking, staring ahead with the knowing smile he usually wore. His look hinted of a hidden secret or sly comment he was about to make. She calls out to him, playfully, but he won't answer.

TURN LEFT

Janice Olson had a strange hobby and a hunch. Her hobby was chasing down wrecked World War II airplanes across the Pacific. Spurred by a personal connection to MIAs (Missing in Action), she regularly took time out of her work schedule to travel the Pacific island battlefields, hunting for clues to missing aircraft and their crews. On this trip in 1994, Olson was following up on a report that had been filed saying that an airplane, possibly American, had been located on a mountainside deep in the New Guinea jungle. A personal ID bracelet with the name "Eberly" stamped on it had been carried out from the site.[132] Olson was the one woman with three men hiking the jungle mountainside, looking for any wreckage they could locate. She had a hunch that they should look in another direction, and she went left, alone, while the others continued on. She thought at the time, *Well, that's no way to cover a lot of ground in a short period of time.* She remembered later, "We were indeed in a jungle, but at 9,000+ altitude in heavy overcast, it was numbingly cold. . . . I was able to find a couple of pieces of the aircraft that had the tail number on them." Number 552 and the remains of her crew, including Tech Sgt. Delmar Dotson, had been found—still manning their posts.

THE RECOVERY

As investigators examined the evidence at the crash site, they pieced together the final moments of the *Listen Here, Tojo!* and her crew. Historian Bruce Hoy stated that the end came abruptly about 11:00 a.m. on September 15, 1943:

The Number 4 engine and right wing tip were torn off by trees growing beside a tributary of the Upper Watut River, as the aircraft was in a tight turn to the right. The rest of it soon came into contact with trees and the terrain, quickly shredding and tearing itself apart. An intense fire broke out in the region of the Number two engine, that consumed a main undercarriage tyre and several fuel tanks. However, due to the separation of the wreckage the fire was limited to this one area.[133]

Wreckage of the Listen Here, Tojo! *#552 can be made out (upside down)*

Memorandum:

DEPARTMENT OF THF ARMY
United States Army Central Identification Laboratory
310 Worchester Avenue
Hickham AFB, Hawaii 96853-5503

TAPC-PED-1-1 (600-8-1 im) 26 October 1994

MEMORANDUM FOR Commander, U.S. Army Central Identification Laboratory, Hawaii, 310 Worchester Avenue, Hickam Air Force Base, HI 96853-5530

SUBJECT: Search and Recovery Report 113/CIL/94, Archaeological Excavation of a B-17F Aircraft Crash Site (MACR #648), Hidden Valley), Upper Watut River, Morobe Province, Papua New Guinea, 4 August–3 September 1993.

The team would wait for the final report, but they already knew. They had found the crew of *Listen Here, Tojo!*. With archaeological methods first perfected in the dust of the lands of the Bible, they excavated, evaluated, and processed their findings with careful precision. They spent thirty-seven days working at the site. Human remains were discovered, so DNA testing would be required for a positive identification. But that would come later. Lt. Howard Eberly's dog tags were at the site. Second Lt. Charles Ranker, the bombardier, was wearing his class ring when the crash occurred, and the ring was at the site. Three ID tags still had legible writing on them, and the names of Eberly, Townsend, and Hall were visible. Fifty years after *Listen Here, Tojo!* had disappeared in a cloud, the team found the crew, still manning their posts. On September 15, 1943, #41-24552, while flying in cloud cover, had crashed into a peak of the Owen Stanley Mountain range. The pilot, Lt. Eberly, may have seen the peak and tried to save the lives of his crew, but they couldn't escape death that time. The remains of the crew were carefully prepared for their journey home.

The military culture of the United States of America is unique in many ways. One distinction concerns the investment in finding and returning the remains of American military personnel who perish overseas. Operating under various names through the years, dedicated professionals track down various clues so that deceased military personnel can be identified and their remains brought back to the United States for burial. At the time of the discovery of the *Listen Here, Tojo!* this unsung unit of heroes was known as the United States Army Central Identification Laboratory.

Excavation photograph—a watch and a pair of goggles from the **Listen Here, Tojo!**

THE PHONE CALL

Once the Central Identification Laboratory had done its work, back in Virginia the Department of the Army's Mortuary Affairs office went to work. Contacting relatives fifty-two years after the fact requires the skills of a detective, and the Mortuary Affairs staff began working through families named Dotson until finally they made a connection with a niece of Delmar's, Brenda Dotson Salyers. Mrs. Saylers informed them that Delmar's little sister, Carrie Lee Nelson, now seventy-five years of age, was living in Maryland. They called Carrie Lee.

Carrie Lee was sitting in her kitchen with her son Jeff and other family members when the phone rang. She had come to terms with her big brother's loss fifty years before, but then came the call. A voice identified herself as a representative of the United States Army and asked if she was speaking to Carrie Lee Dotson Nelson. Carrie Lee told them she was Carrie Lee Dotson Nelson. "We found your brother," the voice said. Carrie Lee was in shock at the news. She said, "Oh my God, I can't believe this! Are you sure? How do you know?"

Genetic testing confirmed what everyone knew. Delmar and the crew of #552 *Listen Here, Tojo!* had been found in the Owen Stanley Mountains, and now he was coming home.

The remains of #41-24552 *Listen Here, Tojo!* still lay on the hillside in the faraway country of New Guinea, a testament that a nation once held certain values worth defending. The men who flew her were valiant warriors of a bygone era.

At 9:00 a.m. on December 11, 1998, T/Sgt. Delmar Dotson and the crew of the *Listen Here, Tojo!* were laid to rest in Arlington National Cemetery with full military honors and with the thanks of a grateful nation. The music that day came from "Pershing's Own" US Army Band. The band's namesake, General John Pershing, had fought with Delmar's 27th Infantry Regiment in the Philippine Insurrection. The caskets carrying the crew on their last journey rode on an army caisson drawn by six horses. The last sounds of the day were, fittingly, those of a trumpet playing taps.[134]

Chaplains were present on that December day to honor the fallen and comfort the families. They spoke to honor the American servicemen and the nation they served. Though their words were fitting and appropriate, perhaps the last word should be from Delmar's own chaplain who wrote to Delmar's mother fifty-five years before the Arlington ceremony:

> If it is found that Divine Providence has embraced your son and his crew from this earth, you can be sure that God will have rendered a just reward for their sacrifice. The teachings of religion assure us that the virtue of Patriotism merits exceedingly with God, and T/Sgt. Dotson in serving his country used his most God-like faculty, free-will, to control his destiny. I pray that God will lessen your uneasiness of mind by resignation to His Will and His Protecting Providence.

Thomas F. Shea
Major C. C. Group Chaplain
October 12, 1943

Technical Sergeant Delmar Dotson, USAAF, 1998

Chapter Twelve:

CONCLUSION

The war over, the living returned to their lives. Some tried to forget their experiences of war, but they were forever changed. Others remembered with pride their service to their country and the comrades in arms who stood with them in the darkest hours.

SONS AND DAUGHTERS OF THE 43RD

The 5th Air Force. Historian Lex McAuley wrote of the exploits of the 5th Air Force, including the 43rd Bombardment Group (H), during 1943–44:

> Its exploits in the South West Pacific have been overshadowed by those in the European Theater. Comparisons are invidious, but a case can be made that the U.S. 5th Air Force, from mid-August 1943 to late April 1944, conducted a campaign of aerial warfare unequaled in World War II in which, despite the severe limitations imposed by weather, terrain, and distance, it repeatedly destroyed the opposing air arm and contributed to the destruction of another at Rabaul.[135]

43rd Bombardment Group (Heavy). Nicknamed "Ken's Men," possibly after 5th Air Force commanding General George Kenney, the unit will remain deployed in the Pacific Theater for the duration of the war. The unit is awarded a Distinguished Unit Citation for the Papua Campaign (1942–43) and a Distinguished Unit Citation for the Battle of the Bismark Sea (1943). They are awarded a Presidential Unit Citation for the Philippines Campaign (1944). The many notable members of the unit include Captain Jay Zeamer, Jr., holder of the Congressional Medal of Honor.[136]

#41-24552 *Listen Here, Tojo!* The plane today rests where she crashed in 1943. She can be found in the appropriately named "Hidden Valley" of the Upper Watut River drainage area at 8,300 feet above sea level in Papua, New Guinea. She was the last B-17 lost in combat in the Pacific theater in World War II.

#41-24552 Listen Here, Tojo! *by Jeremy Clark*

Gray Allison. The 65th Squadron, 43rd Bomb Group (H), flew combat missions up to the end of the war in the Pacific. Allison returned to the United States after the war, married his sweetheart, Voncille, and became a Baptist preacher. He earned a Doctorate in Theology and became a seminary professor and an evangelist. In 1971, he started a school for pastors, church staff members, and missionaries called Mid-America Baptist Theological Seminary. After spending twenty-five years as the school's president, he will retire but continue to teach into his

Dr. B. Gray Allison, President Emeritus, Mid-America Baptist Theological Seminary; B-24 pilot United States Army Air Force

90s. He says that on his tombstone, besides his name, all he wants are "Baptist Preacher" and "US Air Force Pilot."

Anna Clark. The mother of George Stacy, the navigator on the last flight of the *Listen Here, Tojo!* died on September 15, 1963, twenty years to the day after her son's disappearance. She never knew what happened to him.

The Crew of the *Listen Here, Tojo!* Today, Delmar and his crewmates rest at Arlington National Cemetery, section 60. Because they had been declared missing, the names of the crew are engraved in marble at the Manila American Cemetery in the Philippines. The names of the missing-in-action memorialized at the cemetery total 36,285.

The Crew of the Listen Here, Tojo!

Delsie Dotson. Delsie lived to the age of ninety-seven but never knew what happened to her son Delmar. In 1983, she was buried in her hometown of Pound, Virginia, overlooking Mill Creek Road, her home of many years.

Delsie Dotson 1885–1983

153

Ralph Dotson. Ralph Dotson returned from the war changed by his experiences. He pitched professionally in the Chicago Cubs organization for a short time, but a neck injury curtailed his career. He never married but remained a fun-loving member of the Dotson family until his death. He passed away in 1992 on the brink of the discovery of his lost brother Delmar.

Ralph Dotson, somewhere in the Pacific in World War II.

Willie Dotson. Willie returned home to his family after his discharge from the army. His exposure to mustard gas while in his first enlistment caused health issues the rest of his life.

Fannie Elizabeth Simpson Hall. Mother of Watson Hall of the *Listen Here, Tojo!* crew. She saved Watson's high-school letterman's jacket knowing he would return home someday. She told her family that Watson came to her in a vision the night before he died in 1943. She passed away shortly before the *Listen Here, Tojo!* and crew were discovered.[137]

Willie Dotson

Masonic Home of Virginia. The children of the Richmond, Virginia, home are long gone but not forgotten. The facility now houses a retirement community and a masonic library.

Monument to its World War II veterans, Masonic Home of Virginia, 2014.

Max Mayer. 65th Squadron, 43rd Bomb Group (H). A crewmate of Delmar Dotson's on Delmar's Silver-Star mission on April 12, 1943. Mayer enlisted on January 27, 1942, after Pearl Harbor and was soon on his way to the Pacific. Nicknamed "Memphis Max" in New Guinea, he made a career out of the air force, retired as a lieutenant colonel, and moved back home to Memphis, Tennessee. He was active in the 43rd Bomb Group Association until his death in 2008.

His obituary in the *Memphis Commercial Appeal* stated:

MAX HALLE MAYER, 90, retired Air Force Lieutenant Colonel, passed away May 3, 2008 at the Memphis Jewish Home. During World War II he served as a Bombardier Navigator in the South Pacific. He flew 48 missions and earned the Air Medal, Silver Star, Distinguished Flying Cross and many Campaign Medals. In 1951 he was recalled into service and spent 2 years, 7 months in Turkey. He retired from the Air Force in 1968, and was a stock broker for 30 years. Col Mayer was extremely proud of his service to his country and attended many reunions plus Memorial Day and Veterans Day observances locally.[138]

Lt. Col. Max Mayer, Memphis, Tennessee 2015

Emma McCartney. Mother of *Listen Here, Tojo!* gunner Ted McCartney. She lost Ted in 1943, and another son, Bob, was killed at the Battle of the Bulge in 1944. Her hair turned gray overnight. She asked the War Department to send her third son, Chuck, home from Italy, but this was denied because she still had a son at home, fourteen-year-old Bill. She died in 1990 at the age of ninety-six, never knowing what became of her son Ted.

Carrie Lee (Dotson) Nelson. Little sister of Delmar Dotson. Wife of Senator Gaylord Nelson of Wisconsin, she became a fixture on the Washington, D.C., social scene. After the war, she used her position and influence to champion numerous causes, such as environmental protection, and assisted those in need. Tom Brokaw profiled her in his book, *The Greatest Generation.*

Janice Olson. After assisting with the recovery of the *Listen Here, Tojo!* she continued working to identify missing wrecks in the Pacific. Upon returning from New Guinea and the crash site of the *Listen Here, Tojo!* she returned Lt. Howard Eberly's ID bracelet to his widow fifty years after her husband's disappearance.

Carrie Lee Nelson, Delmar's little sister

Tsgt Delmar Dotson, 1916–1943. Inscribed to his sister Laura Dotson Spradlin.

Selected Bibliography

BOOKS

Addington, Luther F. *The Story of Wise County (Virginia)*. Published by Centennial Committee and School Board of Wise County, Virginia. 1956.

Barr, James A. *Airpower Employment of the Fifth Air Force in the World War II Southwest Pacific Theater*. ebook Edition, Pickle Partners Publishing, 2014. www.picklepartnerspublishing.com, 2014. Originally published in 1997.

Baumgardner, Randy, ed. *Fifth Air Force*. Turner Publishing Company: Paducah, KY, 1994.

Bergerund, Eric M. *Fire in the Sky: The Air War in the South Pacific*. Westview Press: Boulder, CO, 2000.

Birdsall, Steve. *Fighting Colors: B-17 Flying Fortress in Color*. Illustrated by Don Greer. Squadron Signal Publications: Carrollton, TX, 1986.

Birdsall, Steve. *Flying Buccaneers: The Illustrated Story of Kenney's Fifth Air Force*. With a Foreword by General George C. Kenney. Doubleday & Company: Garden City, New York, 1977.

Birdsall, Steve. *Pride of Seattle: The First 300 Boeing B-17F Flying Fortresses*. Squadron/Signal Publications, Inc.: Carrollton, TX, 1998.

Blair, Frederick. *Down Under: 50 Year Special Edition, The 43rd Bomb Group in New Guinea and Australia*. Halstead Press Publishers: New South Wales, Australia, 1994. Reprint ed. *Down Under: The 43rd Bomb Group in New Guinea and Australia*. Angus and Robertson: Sydney, 1943.

SONS OF THE 43RD

Bowman, Martin. *B-17 Flying Fortress Units of the Pacific War.* Osprey Combat Aircraft 39. Osprey Publishing: Oxford, 2003.

Bozung, Jack, ed. *The Fifth over the Southwest Pacific.* AAF Publications Company: Los Angeles, CA, n.d.

Bradley, Phillip. *The Battle for Wau: New Guinea's Frontline 1942–43.* Cambridge University Press, 2008.

Bruning, John R. *Jungle Ace: Col. Gerald R. Johnson, the USAAF's Top Fighter Leader of the Pacific War.* Brassey's, Inc.: Washington, DC, 2001.

Claringbold, Michael John. *The Forgotten Fifth: A Photographic Chronology of the U.S. Fifth Air Force in WW2.* Balus Productions: New York, 2007.

Conner, H. T., Delores Harris Conner, Wayne Donahoe, Liz Morris Meador, Marie Morris Barnett, William Gilbert Morris; with the contribution of other Home Kids. *History of the Masonic Home of Virginia: Between 1890 and 1975 When It Served Children and Youth.* Members of the Masonic Home Alumni Association: Richmond, VA, 2013.

Cooper, Anthony. *Kokoda Air Strikes: Allied Air Forces in New Guinea, 1942.* ebook Edition. NewSouth Publishing, University of New South Wales Press, Ltd.: Sydney, NSW, Australia, 2014. www.newsouthpublishing.com.

Crawford, William, Jr. *Gore and Glory: A Story of American Heroism.* As told to Ted Saucier. David McKay Company: Philadelphia, 1944. Reprinted by Kingsport Press: Kingsport, TN, n.d.

Cutler, Robert S. *A History of the Fifth Air Force's Worst Air Crash in World War II.* Pacific Air Forces, Office of History: Hickam Air Force Base, Hawaii, 2003.

Darby, Charles. *Pacific Wrecks and Where to Find Them.* Kookaburra Technical Publications Pty Ltd.: Melbourne, Australia: 1979.

Dorr, Robert F. *B-24 Liberator Units of the Pacific War.* Osprey Combat Aircraft 11, Tony Holmes, series editor. Osprey Publishing: Oxford, United Kingdom, 1999.

Dotson, Rena Meade. *Stitches in Time: Rena Remembers-A Memoir.* Edited by Brenda D. Salyers, Helen Dotson, and Lynda Hubbard. Pound, Virginia: Heritage Nook Books, 2010.

Edwards, Grace B. and Brenda D. Salyers, eds. *The History of the Pound, Volumes I–III: People of the Pound.* Pound, VA: The Historical Society of the Pound, 1996.

Ethell, Jeffrey. *B-17 Flying Fortress.* Warbirds Illustrated no. 41. Arms and Armour Press, Ltd.: London, 1986.

Frederick, Clinton. *Word War II: A Legacy of Letters, One Soldier's Journey.* Zonicom Press, LLC: Scottsdale, AZ, 2006.

Gailey, Harry A. *The War in the Pacific: From Pearl Harbor to Tokyo Bay.* Presidio Press: Novato, CA, 1995.

Gallagher, James P. *With the Fifth Air Force: Photos from the Pacific Theater.* Foreword by Eric Bergerund. The Johns Hopkins University Press: Baltimore, 2001.

Gamble, Bruce. *Fortress Rabaul: The Battle for the Southwest Pacific January 1942–April 1943.* Zenith Press: Minneapolis, MN, 2010.

Gannon, Michael. *Operation Drumbeat: The Dramatic True Story of Germany's First U-Boat Attacks Along the American Coast in World War II.* Harper Collins e-books: New York, 2010.

Guy, Sallie. *Flying Without Wings: The Story of Carroll Guy: A World War II Bomber Pilot.* Indianapolis, Indiana: Dog Ear Publishing, 2007.

Hastings, Max. *Retribution: The Battle for Japan, 1944-45.* Alfred A. Knopf: New York, 2008.

Haugland, Vern. *The AAF against Japan*. Harper & Brothers Publishers: New York, 1948.

Hipps, William, Francis Gideon, Benjamin Cain, and William E. Johnson. *The Fifth Air Force in the War against Japan*. The United States Strategic Bombing Survey. Military Analysis Division: Washington, DC, 1947.

Jablonski, Edward. *The Illustrated Biography of the B-17s and the Men Who Flew Them*. Doubleday & Company, Inc.: Garden City, New York, 1965.

King, Dan. *The Last Zero Fighter: Firsthand Accounts from WWII Japanese Naval Pilots*. ebook Edition. Pacific Press: Irvine, CA. Revised Edition April 30, 2013. First Published July 11, 2012. Author Copyright 2012. www.historicalconsulting.com.

Kohn, Richard H. and Joseph P. Harahan, eds. *USAF Warrior Studies: General Kenney Reports, A Personal History of the Pacific War*, by George C. Kenney. Reprinted by Office of Air Force History. Washington, D.C.: United States Air Force, 1987.

Lardner, John. *Southwest Passage: The Yanks in the Pacific*. J. B. Lippincott Company, Philadelphia, 1943.

Lundstrom, John B. *The First South Pacific Campaign: Pacific Fleet Strategy December 1941–June 1942*. ebook Edition. Naval Institute Press: Annapolis, MD, 1976. Kindle Edition.

Mayo, Lida. *Bloody Buna: The Grueling Campaign in New Guinea that Thwarted the Japanese Invasion of Australia*. Doubleday and Company, Inc.: Garden City, NY, 1974.

McAulay, Lex. *Into the Dragon's Jaws: The U.S. Fifth Air Force at Rabaul October-November 1943*. ebook Edition. Banner Books, Maryborough, Queensland, Australia, 2012. www.banner-books.com.au.

McAulay, Lex. *MacArthur's Eagles: The U. S. Air War Over New Guinea 1943–44*. Naval Institute Press: Annapolis, MD, 2005.

McNeely, Gina and Jon Guttman. *War in the Pacific: Pearl Harbor to Hiroshima—The Pacific War in 400 Color Photographs*. Metro Books: New York, New York, 2011.

Milner, Samuel. *Victory in Papua*. In *United States Army in World War II: The War in the Pacific*. Kent Roberts Greenfield, General Editor. Office of the Chief of Military History, Department of the Army: Washington, DC, 1957.

Moore, Sidney C., Jr. and the Associated Press. *War Against Japan*. Presidio Press: Novato, CA. 1994.

Morison, Samuel Eliot. *Breaking the Bismark Barrier: 22 July 1942-1 May 1944*. Vol. 6 of *History of United States Naval Operations in World War II*. With an Introduction by Vincent P. O'Hara. Naval Institute Press, Annapolis, Maryland, 1950.

Null, Gary. *Weapon of Denial: Air Power and the Battle for New Guinea*. ebook Edition. Pickle Partners Publishing, 2015. www.picklepartnerspublishing.com, Original Edition published in 1995.

Paloque, Gerard. *The 5th Air Force*. Translated from the French by Lawrence Brown. Histoire et Collections: Paris, France, 2009.

Rems, Alan. *South Pacific Cauldron: World War II's Great Forgotten Battlegrounds*. ebook Edition. Naval Institute Press: Annapolis, MD, 2014.

Reynolds, Quentin. *70,000 to 1: The Story of Lieutenant Gordon Manuel*. Pyramid Books: New York, 1968.

Robertson, Rhonda and Nancy Clark Brown, eds. *The History of the Pound*. Volume I. The Historical Society of the Pound: n.p., 1993.

Rodman, Matthew K. *A War of Their Own: Bombers over the Southwest Pacific.* Air University Press: Maxwell Air Force Base, Alabama, 2005.

Rust, Kenn C. *Fifth Air Force Story . . . in World War II.* Historical Aviation Album: Temple City, CA, 1973.

Salecker, Gene Eric. *Fortress Against the Sun: The B-17 Flying Fortress in the Pacific.* Combined Publishing: Conshohocken, PA, 2001.

Salyers, Brenda. *Branhams and Kin: The Descendants of Milly Branham.* Pound, VA: Heritage Nook Books Publishing, n.d.

Scott Field: Army Air Forces Technical Training Command, A Pictorial and Historical Review of Scott Field. Everett Schneider Co. St. Louis, MO, n.d.

Simons, Graham M. and Harry Friedman. *Boeing B-17: The Fifteen Ton Flying Fortress.* South Yorkshire, Barnsley, Great Britain, 2011.

Sinton, Russell L. *The Menace from Moresby.* The Battery Press: Nashville, TN, 1989.

Stava, Robert J. *Combat Recon: 5th Air Force Images from the SW Pacific 1943– 45.* Schiffer Military History: Atglen, PA, 2007.

Stories from the Fifth Air Force: A Collection of Tales from Southwest Pacific Bomb Groups Retold by International Historical Research Associates. ebook Edition, International Historical Research Associates: No Place. Kindle Edition, 2015. ISBN 978-0-913511-10-7.

Taafe, Stephen R. *MacArthur's Jungle War: The 1944 New Guinea Campaign.* University Press of Kansas: Lawrence, KS, 1998.

Taggart, William C. and Christopher Cross. *My Fighting Congregation.* Doubleday, Doran, and Company, Inc.: Garden City, NY, 1943.

Tillman, Barrett. *Whirlwind: The Air War Against Japan 1942-1945*. Simon & Schuster: New York, 2010.

Vaughn, Robert V. *In the Shadow of Trinity: An American Airman in Occupied Japan*. Sunflower University Press: Manhattan, KS, 1991.

Weaver, Jeffrey C. *The Civil War in Buchanan and Wise Counties: Bushwacker's Paradise*. H. E. Howard: Lynchburg, VA, 1994.

Wistrand, R. B., ed. *Pacific Sweep: A Pictorial History of the Fifth Air Force Fighter Command*. F. H. Johnston Publishing Company: Sydney, Australia, n.d.

Wright, J. L. *The Search that Never Was: The Untold Truth about the 1948-49 Search for World War II American Personnel Missing in Action in the South Pacific*. Strategic Book Publishing and Rights Co.: Houston, TX, 2014.

PERIODICALS

Aukofer, Frank A. "Coming Home: Bomber Crew Given Final Rest." *Milwaukee Journal Sentinel*. December 11, 1998.

Burns, St. Claire. "Abbeville Soldier Laid to Rest More than 50 Years after His Death in WWII," *The Index-Journal*, May 31, 1999.

Cohn, Art. "Z Is for Zeamer." *Liberty Magazine*. Edward Maher, ed. January 15, 1944. Pp. 22-23, 69.

Hoy, Bruce. "Listen Here, Tojo!" *Australian Military History*. Vol. 1. April-May 1994:16-19.

Hutton, Geoffrey. "Fortress Home with 4 Wounded: Attacked by 9 Zeros," *The Argus*, Thursday March 11, 1943. Reprinted from The National Library of Australia. http://nla.gov.au/nla

Johnston, George. "'Out There': Damn War's Gone Old Fashioned in Steamy Jungles of New Guinea." *Life*. January 4, 1943, pp. 22-24.

"Max Halle Mayer," *Commercial Appeal*. Obituary section archives. www. legacy.com.

"A Nightmare Flight: Desperate Task to Release Bomb" The West Australian (Tuesday 22 June 1943), p. 3. Reprinted from The National Library of Australia. http://nla.gov.au/nla.news-article46760316.

"Pound Soldier Wins Silver Star Fighting Japs," *Kingsport Times*, Monday August 30, 1943. Reprinted in www.newspapers.com www. newspapers.com/image/74760047.

Richmond Times-Dispatch, various dates.

REFERENCE WORKS

Aldebol, Anthony. *Decorations, Medals, Ribbons, Badges and Insignia of the United States Air Force: The First 50 Years*. Medals of America Series. MOA (Medals of America Press): Fountain Inn, SC, 1997.

Hammel, Eric. *Air War Pacific: America's Air War against Japan in East Asia and the Pacific 1941–1945: Chronology*. Pacifica Press: Pacifica, CA, 1998.

Maurer, Maurer, ed. *Combat Squadrons of the Air Force: World War II*. USAF Historical Division, Air University, Department of the Air Force, US Government Printing Office: Washington, DC, 1969.

Random House World Atlas and Encyclopedia. S.v. "Papua New Guinea." Random House Reference: New York, 2007.

Watkins, Robert A. *Battle Colors: Insignia and Aircraft Markings of the U.S. Army Air Forces of World War II*. Volume V Pacific Theater of Operations. Schiffer Publishing, Ltd.: Atglen, PA, 2013.

UNPUBLISHED MATERIALS

"History of the 43rd Bombardment Group (H) Period (15 January 1941 to 29 February 1944)." 43rd Bombardment Group (H), V Bomber Command, 5th Air Force, United States Army. Roll #BO 135. Date Filmed: 2-1-73. Maxwell AFB, Alabama. Declassified 1 June 1959.

"History of the 43rd Bombardment Group (H) Period (June 1945 to September 1945)." 43rd Bombardment Group (H), V Bomber Command, 5th Air Force, United States Army. Roll #BO 136. Date Filmed: 2-1-73. Maxwell AFB, Alabama. Declassified 1 June 1959.

A Pocket Guide to New Guinea and the Solomons. Prepared by Special Service Division, Army Service Forces, United States Army in Cooperation with the Office of Strategic Services. Washington, DC: War and Navy Departments.

Weekly Status Reports of the 43rd Bombardment Group. Archives of the Air Force Historical Research Agency (AFHRA). Maxwell Air Force Base.

Weekly Status Reports of the 63rd Squadron, 43rd Bombardment Group. Archives of the Air Force Historical Research Agency (AFHRA). Maxwell Air Force Base.

Weekly Status Reports of the 64th Squadron, 43rd Bombardment Group. Archives of the Air Force Historical Research Agency (AFHRA). Maxwell Air Force Base.

Weekly Status Reports of the 65th Squadron, 43rd Bombardment Group. Archives of the Air Force Historical Research Agency (AFHRA). Maxwell Air Force Base.

Endnotes

CHAPTER ONE

1 Grace B. Edwards and Brenda D. Salyers, *The History of the Pound*, vol. III (Pound, VA: The Historical Society of the Pound, 1996), pp. 3-57.

2 Jeff Weaver, *The Civil War in Buchanan and Wise Counties: Bushwacker's Paradise* (H. E. Howard: Lynchburg, VA, 1994). See also: *Highland Echo*, vol. 11, March 1993, no. 40 and *Highland Echo*, vol. 12, March 1994, no. 44 (www.geocitiessites.com, s.v. "Alf Killen")

3 Luther F. Addington, *The Story of Wise County (Virginia)*. Published by Centennial Committee and School Board of Wise County, Virginia. 1956, pp. 109-110. See also Jeff Weaver's *The Civil War in Buchanan and Wise Counties—Bushwacker's Paradise*.

4 Lola Dotson personal memories and notes. Author's collection. See Also: Brenda Salyer's *Branhams and Kin: The Descendants of Milly Branham*.

5 Brenda Salyers, *Branhams and Kin: the Descendants of Milly Branham*. (Pound, Virginia: Heritage Nook Books, n.d.), pp. 36-38.

6 Rhonda Robertson and Nancy Clark Brown, eds., *The History of the Pound*, vol. I, (n.p.: Historical Society of the Pound, 1993), pp. 398-400.

7 Rena Meade Dotson, *Stitches in Time: Rena Remembers-A Memoir*. Edited by Brenda D. Salyers, Helen Dotson, and Lynda Hubbard, (Pound, VA: Heritage Nook Books, 2010), p. 106.

8 Addington, p. 203.

9 Rena Meade Dotson, p. 106.

CHAPTER TWO

10 H. T. Conner, Delores Harris Conner, Wayne Donahoe, Liz Morris Meador, Marie Morris Barnett, William Gilbert Morris; with the contribution of other Home Kids, *History of the Masonic Home of Virginia: Between 1890 and 1975 When It Served Children and Youth*. (Richmond, VA: Members of the Masonic Home Alumni Association, 2013), p. 354. Hereafter cited as *Masonic Home*.

11   *Masonic Home*, pp. 1-11.

12   Oral recording of Delsie Dotson. Author's Collection.

13   *Masonic Home*, p. 400.

14   *Masonic Home*, p. 345.

15   *Masonic Home*, p. 75.

16   Interview with the Author, July 2013, Kensington, MD.

17   Interview with the Author, July 2013, Kensington, MD.

18   *Masonic Home*, pp. 78, 282.

19   *Masonic Home*, pp. 128-129.

20   *Masonic Home*, pp. 359-361.

21   Tom Wiley, *Richmond Times-Dispatch*, November 29, 1936, p. 6.

22   *Masonic Home*, p. 360.

23   *Masonic Home*, p. 347.

24   *Richmond Times-Dispatch*, June 17, 1934, p. 8.

25   Rena Meade Dotson, p. 111.

26   Delmar's older sister Laura (now Spradlin) left her family in Radnor, Ohio, to come to Virginia and care for Delsie and Virgil, possibly during their recuperation from this accident. Laura returned home at the end of July, and as she got off the bus, a man said, "So sorry for your loss, Mrs. Spradlin." It was the first that she had heard of her two-year-old son Bobby's death. She had missed the telegram of her child's demise to whooping cough while travelling. She and her husband were too poor to erect a headstone, and the grave remained unmarked until 2014.

27   *Richmond Times-Dispatch*, November 11, 1934, p. 5.

28   *Richmond Times-Dispatch*, November 17, 1934, p. 11.

29   *Richmond Times-Dispatch*, November 26, 1935, p. 20.

30 *Richmond Times-Dispatch*, November 7, 1937, p. 4.

31 Tom Wiley, *Richmond Times-Dispatch*, November 29, 1936, p. 6.

CHAPTER THREE

32 Personal Correspondence with the Author.

33 Salyers, p. 57.

34 "WASHINGTON, July 12, 2013 – Forty years ago today, an enormous fire erupted at the National Personnel Records Center in suburban St. Louis. Burning uncontrollably for almost 24 hours, it destroyed some 16 million to 18 million military personnel records including official documents veterans need to apply for the benefits they've earned." The Article adds, "The July 12, 1973, fire destroyed up to 80 percent of the 22 million records of veterans of the Army, Army Air Force and Air Force who served between 1912 and 1963, reported William Seibert, senior archivist and chief of archival operations at the National Archives in St. Louis. About 85 percent of the records of soldiers discharged between 1912 and 1959, including veterans of World War II and the Korean War, went up in smoke. In addition, about 75 percent of the records of airmen with last names beginning with "H" through "Z" who left service between 1947 and 1963 were lost." Donna Miles, "Experts Recover Military Personnel Records Forty Years After Fire," American Forces Press Service, U. S. Department of Defense, July 13, 2013, www.defense.gov

35 James Jones, *From Here to Eternity*, edited and with an afterward by George Hendrick (New York: Open Road Integrated Media, ebook edition, n.d.), p. 10.

36 Maj. A. E. O'Flaherty, Jr., editor, *The Bark of the 27th U. S. Infantry Wolfhounds* (Signal Corps U. S. Army, Schofield Studio, 1941), p. 4-5.

37 Maj. A. E. O'Flaherty, Jr., editor, *The Bark of the 27th U. S. Infantry Wolfhounds* (Signal Corps U. S. Army, Schofield Studio, 1941), p. 3.

38 Tropic Lightening Museum information. http:// www.garrison.hawaii.army. mil/tlm/

39 *A History of U.S. Army Bands*, subcourse number MU0010, edition D (Norfolk, VA: US Army Element, School of Music), p. 13.

40 Maj. A. E. O'Flaherty, Jr., editor, *The Bark of the 27th U. S. Infantry Wolfhounds* (Signal Corps U. S. Army, Schofield Studio, 1941), p. 6.

41 *Activities in Schofield Barracks Hawaii*, (U.S. Signal Corps, U. S. Army, n.p.), pp. 2-3.

42 Information from the Tropic Lightning Museum states that Miss Temple's appearance with the 27th Infantry Regiment band took place in 1935. Tropic Lightning Museum, 350 Eastman Road, Schofield Bks, HI 96857. Local newspapers place the visit in the years 1937 or 1939.

43 Harry B. Soria, Jr., Correspondence with the Author, July 22, 2015.

CHAPTER FOUR

44 Rena Meade Dotson, p. 112.

45 Robert I. Curtis, John Mitchell, and Martin Copp, *Langley Field, The Early Years: 1916-1946*, Langley AFB, Virginia: Office of History 450oth Air Base Wing, 1977), p. 102.

46 1st Indorsement [sic] to Inspector General Inspection, Langley Field, Va., 5 April 1940, 17 June 1940 SD 36 to HLF, 1 Mar 35 to 7 Dec 41, p. 25. Quoted in Curtis, Mitchell, and Copp, p. 135.

47 Curtis, Mitchell, Copp, p. 105.

48 Curtis, Mitchell, Copp, p. 148.

49 *The Times Recorder* (Zanesville, Ohio), 16 December 1941, p. 2.

50 "The Foundations of a War Training Program, Chapter 14, p. 455. www.ibiblio.org/hyperwar/aaf/vi/aaf-vi-14.html

51 Military Yearbook Project Website: http://militaryyearbookproject.com/references/old-mos-codes/wwii-era/army-wwii-codes/gunnery-and-gunnery-control/airplane-mechanic-gunner-748

52 43rd Bombardment Group History, (Maxwell Air Force Base, Montgomery. Alabama: Air Force Historical Association), Roll BO-135.

CHAPTER FIVE

53 Edward Jablonski, *Flying Fortress: The Illustrated Biography of the B-17s and the Men Who Flew Them,* (Garden City, New York: Doubleday & Company, Inc., 1965), pp. 5-6.

54 Jablonski, pp. 32-34.

55   Graham M. Simons and Dr. Harry Friedman, *The Boeing B-17: '...The Fifteen Ton Flying Fortress,'* (Barnsley, South Yorkshire, Great Britain: Pen and Sword Books Ltd, 2011), pp. 101-107.

56   Graham M. Simons and Harry Friedman. *Boeing B-17: The Fifteen Ton Flying Fortress* (South Yorkshire, Barnsley, Great Britain: n.p., 2011), p. 107.

57   "41-24552" Dave Osborne, "B-17 Fortress Master Log." www.americanairmuseum.com.

58   Simons and Friedman, p. 117.

CHAPTER SIX

59   "History of the 43rd Bombardment Group (H) Period (15 January 1941 to 29 February 1944)." 43rd Bombardment Group (H), V Bomber Command, 5th Air Force, United States Army. Roll #BO 135. Date Filmed: 2-1-73. Maxwell AFB, Alabama. Declassified 1 June 1959. Hereafter cited as "43rd Bomb Group Roll #."

60   43rd Bomb Group History, Roll B135

61   Ken's Men Newsletter, July 1998, p. 8.

62   43rd Bomb Group History, Roll B135

63   Dotson, Delmar, IDPF: Individual Deceased Personnel File.

64   Unit Histories cited by Salecker, pp. 159-161.

65   Ken's Men Newsletter, July 2011, pp. 7-9. "Recollections of col. Pettus."

66   R. B. Wistrand, editor, *Pacific Sweep: A Pictorial History of the Fifth Air Force Fighter Command,* (F. H. Johnson Publishing company: Sydney, Australia, n.d.), p. 24.

67   Lex McAuley, *MacArthur's Eagles: The U. S. Air War over New Guinea 1943-44,* (Annapolis, MD: Naval Institute Press, 2005), p. 31.

68   Michael Parrish, DDS, Memphis, Tennessee. Correspondence with the Author, July 2, 2014.

69   Roy Hodkinson, reprinted on www.ozatwar.com, "Townsville @ War."

70   Bruce Hoy, "Listen Here Tojo." *Australian Military History*. Vol. 1. April-May 1994:16-19. See Also: www.pacificwrecks.com as an excellent source of information on the 43rd.

71   Eric M. Bergerund, *Fire in the Sky: The Air War in the South Pacific.* (Boulder, CO: Westview Press, 2000), p. 61.

72   Eric Bergurund, *Fire in the Sky*, p. 61.

73   Richard H. Kohn and Joseph P. Harahan, eds. *USAF Warrior Studies: General Kenney Reports, A Personal History of the Pacific War*, by. George C. Kenney. Reprinted by Office of Air Force History (Washington, D.C.: United States Air Force, 1987), pp. 105, 152. Hereafter cited as General Kenney Reports.

74   George Johnston, "'Out There': Damn War's Gone Old Fashioned in Steamy Jungles of New Guinea." *Life*, January 4, 1943, pp. 22-24.

75   http://www.powens.com/MAINREPT.htm

76   General Kenney Reports, pp. 40-41.

77   General Kenney Reports, p. 185.

78   General Kenney Reports, pp. xi-xii.

79   General Kenney Reports, p. 11.

80   General Kenney Reports, pp. 56-57.

81   Lex McAuley, *MacArthur's Eagles*, pp. 188, 191.

82   General Kenney Reports, pp. 141-142.

83   Hoy, pp. 16-17. See also Weekly Status Reports of the 65th Squadron.

84   Salecker, p. 273.

85   Bergerund, p. 146.

86   *A Pocket Guide to New Guinea and the Solomons.* Prepared by Special Service Division, Army Service Forces, United States Army in Cooperation with the Office of Strategic Services. Washington, D.C.: War and Navy Departments, pp. 2-3.

87 *Pocket Guide*, pp. 57-63.

88 "A Nightmare Flight: Desperate Task to Release Bomb" *The West Australian* (Tuesday 22 June 1943), p. 3. Reprinted from The National Library of Australia. http://nla.gov.au/nla.news-article46760316.

89 Bergerund, p. 24.

90 General Kenney Reports, p. 226.

91 Geoffrey Hutton, "Fortress Home with 4 Wounded: Attacked by 9 Zeros," *The Argus*, Thursday March 11, 1943, p. 4. Reprinted from The National Library of Australia. http://nla.gov.au/nla

92 Sallie Guy, *Flying Without Wings: The Story of Carroll Guy: A World War II Bomber Pilot*, (Indianapolis, IN: Dog Ear Publishing, 2007), pp. 46-47.

CHAPTER SEVEN

93 Bergerund, p. 317.

94 Hoy, p. 17.

95 Weekly Status Report for February 1, 43rd Bomb Group, Unit History.

96 Hoy, p. 18.

97 Hoy, p. 18.

98 Weekly Status and Operations Report of the 65th Squadron, Week of March 28-April 4, 1943. Sq-bomb-su 44273

99 William Crawford and Ted Sacier, *Gore and Glory: A Story of American Heroism*, (Philadelphia, PA: David McKay Company, 1944), reprinted by Kingsport Press, Inc., Kingsport, TN, n.d., p. 133.

100 Crawford, pp. 136-138.

101 Crawford, pp. 138-140.

102 "Pound Soldier Wins Silver Star Fighting Japs," *Kingsport Times*, Monday August 30, 1943. Reprinted in www.newspapers.com , http://www.newspapers.com/image/74760047.

Chapter Eight

103 Hoy, p. 17

104 Hoy, p. 18.

105 Letter from Chaplain (Maj.) Thomas F. Shea to Delsie Dotson, October 12, 1943. Author's Collection.

106 General Kenney Reports, pp. 193-194.

107 General Kenney Reports, p. 229.

108 Hoy, p. 17. See Also Marcia Brenneman, *Walter: An Airman's Life*, (New Paris, Indiana: The Farmer's Exchange Co., 1989), pp. 203-205.

109 Russell L. Sinton, compiler, *The Menace from Moresby*, (Nashville, TN: The Battery Press, 1989), n.p. Under the heading, "Excerpts from a Jap Diary."

110 Marcia Brenneman, pp. 196-197.

111 www.kensmen.com, listing of the B-17s that served in the 43rd Bomb Group.

112 Hoy, p. 17.

113 General Kenney Reports, pp. 235-236.

Chapter Nine

114 Marcia Brenneman, pp. 218-220.

115 Hoy, p. 18.

116 Bill Heltzel, "Gunner at Peace," *Pittsburg Post-Gazette*, December 7, 1998, p. 10.

117 "Abbeville Soldiers Missing in Action," *The Index-Journal* (Greenwood, South Carolina), Sept. 24, 1943, p. 5.

118 www.powens.my.cape.com

119 Dotson, Delmar *Individual Deceased Personnel File*

120 Ken's Men Newsletter, October 1995, p. 4. See also Ken's Men Newsletter, January 1996, p. 2.

CHAPTER TEN

121 *TS: The Voice of the GI-43rd Bomb Group*, vol. 1 No. 2 19 Feb. '45.

122 James A. Patterson, *To All the World: A History of Mid-America Baptist Theological Seminary, 1972-1997* (Memphis, TN: Disciple Design, 1997), pp. 10-14.

123 Log notes, personal papers of Dr. Gray Allison

124 Ken's Men Newsletter September 1986, p. 3.

125 General Kenney Reports, p. 541.

126 Robert V. Vaughn, *In the Shadow of Trinity: An American Airman in Occupied Japan,* (Sunflower University Press: Manhattan, KS), p. 33.

127 B. Gray Allison, "The Man of God," printed in *Baptist Trumpet: Official Publication of Baptist Missionary Association of Arkansas*, May 8, 2002, pp. 1-4.

128 General Kenney, p. 122.

129 www.kensmen.com s.v. "The Fifth Air Force in WWII: August 1945"

130 Delmar Dotson, *Individual Deceased Personnel File*

131 Gen. Kenney Reports, pp. 354-357.

CHAPTER ELEVEN

132 This may be what one veteran called a "crash tag." A crash tag was an ID bracelet made by local craftsman. Some airmen felt that if they died in a fire the "crash tag," or ID bracelet, would help identify them. See: William C. Taggart and Christopher Cross, *My Fighting Congregation* (Doubleday, Doran, and Company, Inc., 1943), pp. 77-78.

133 Hoy, pp. 18-19.

CHAPTER TWELVE

134 Frank A. Aukofer, "Coming Home: Bomber Crew Given Final Rest." *Milwaukee Journal Sentinel.* December 11, 1998.

135 Lex McAuley, *MacArthur's Eagles*, p. 251.

136 Two excellent resources are the websites for the 43rd Bomb Group (www.kenismen.com) and Pacific Wrecks (www.pacificwrecks.com)

137 St. Claire Burns, "Abbeville Soldier Laid to Rest More than 50 Years after His Death in WWII," *The Index-Journal*, May 31, 1999, p.1.

138 "Max Halle Mayer," *Commercial Appeal.* Obituary section archives. www.legacy.com.

Made in the USA
Middletown, DE
18 December 2021

56522918R00099